Speaking Human

Speaking Human

The Tragedy of the Retarded Genius

Adrienne Fergessen

Library of Congress Control Number:		2016912610
ISBN:	Hardcover	978-1-5245-1599-7
	Softcover	978-1-5245-1598-0
	eBook	978-1-5245-1600-0

Print information available on the last page.

Rev. date: 08/07/2017

To order additional copies of this book, contact:
Xlibris
1-800-455-039
www.Xlibris.com.au
Orders@Xlibris.com.au
513753

Aunty Sabrina was the most successful woman I knew in Australia, and if I were going to get a job, I was asking for help. She promised to take time out to help me soon, but in the meantime, she knew of someone who would be happy to take me on in an admin role.

She said his name was Jamiel Levant, and after Aunty Sabrina gave me the okay, I called to hear a very polite, articulate, and clear voice. It wasn't long before Jamiel was organising for me to meet the manager, Micah.

Micah was an awkward fellow; a very tall, solid, hobo-like, no eye contact, very low-voiced, anti-manager who was very kind when explaining the ropes to me. This lasted for about an hour before the most gorgeous man I had ever seen in real life—okay maybe not the most gorgeous, but he was really, really good looking—with his white V-neck shirt that hugged his upper body quite nicely, showing a physique that was very pleasing to the eye.

I decided I should shake this guy's hand as the normal office thing to do. He asked me what my plans were for my future as I shared my dream to graduate as a pharmacist to open a string of stores someday. I hoped I could keep this job, as I was good at Excel and no other business would hire me without experience—and I really needed some experience so I could be hired as someone with experience. A very tall man, a confident guy showing no signs of being strange—I hoped my boyfriend wouldn't see my ear-to-ear grin after work.

Christmas came along and the manager, Micah, was tolerating this Jamiel guy quite nicely, despite Micah's staff member's quirks becoming more obvious to me. He didn't seem to see the 'Don't lean on the bikes' sign as he leaned his large frame on them, and he perhaps seemed not to be entirely with us between saying almost the exact same lines to each customer as he would book them sports cars to hire, one after another. His charming exterior was almost as that of a programmed robot, but he must have been doing well for Micah to have kept him on the team all this time.

'Good morning, Rennie'—a message appeared at my work Skype window.

'How did you know that was my nickname?' I replied.

'That's what Sabrina calls you,' he replied. Fair enough.

He would wish me a good morning and good evening each day from then on via Skype and I would reply in kind, with his quirkiness more comfortable spending time with us, saying the strangest of things that seemed to have no relationship to reality. Until that day it was pouring rain and he was leaving in his dad's car with his DJ gear before noticing that I may need a lift out of the rain. On the way home, I had finally decided that this guy was weird.

I asked him who he was planning on voting for in the upcoming elections since I had finally reached voting age.

He didn't believe in voting.

'Why?'

'Maybe I'll tell you later.'

'But I want to know now.'

He then gave me this weird arse answer that I wasn't even sure was in English.

I replied with my usual, dry wit. 'That makes perfect sense.'

'Thank you!' he replied, completely missing the sarcasm of the comment.

Now I was sure he was weird.

'Don't you think that the frequency with which your mother contacts you throughout the day at least slightly deviates from the mean?' he asked me one afternoon whilst getting the now regular trip home with Jamiel.

'Huh?' I had no idea what he was on about. 'Speak English, please, Jamiel. My brain has had a long day at work.'

'Sorry.' He was always polite in monotone, having the usual lack of idea about how he had not gotten his message across. As was now more common, I helped him speak human.

'I think you mean to say that you think my mum calls me too much, right?'

'No,' he replied. 'I meant to say what I said, but perhaps I could clarify by saying that the space between phone calls has been averaging six minutes. My question to you is what could change in six minutes that would necessitate a mother needing to verify her adult daughter's well-being?'

I think he was trying to say that it was weird that my mum called me so much. He was, as always, kind enough to let me work it out on my own, and within a few days I did realise that six minutes per missed call was kinda strange.

A few rides home later and he asked me why I said my dad was dead with no fluctuation in my tone of voice as compared to my usually excited tone.

'The equations I have used to construct your character suggest to me that your dad is still alive and that for some reason you don't want to talk about it.'

He was right. I didn't want to talk about it, but of course, the subject was now open.

'Okay. Fine. He is still alive.' His next comment still threw me off.

'I already know that he is still alive, but why is it fine?' His weirdness had to be put on the side for now, as how in the hell did he know he was still alive and why did it matter?

'How—'

Then he interrupted me immediately.

'It isn't important how I know, but more important that you know why you feel the need to cover this with a bullshit story. I'm assuming you do this in general, but as per my understanding of humans, no one has likely pulled you up on your lie.'

'You are very strange' came out of my mouth before my brain had a chance to stop it.

'I have been told that before,' he replied, 'and once I tell you about my life, it may make more sense. In the meantime, however, keep thinking about why your mother would contact you so often and why you need to believe your dad is dead.' He dropped me off to a screaming mother while I used all my mental power to block her out whilst looking forward to seeing my baby half-brother after his first day at school.

Days passed, with not much conversation between us until a Skype message came through:

> Jamiel: Why aren't you sending your emails to me to be checked before sending them out?
> Adrienne: Why should I? Who are you? Micah checks my emails.
> Jamiel: But I check Micah's emails.
> Adrienne: Why would you check his emails?
> Jamiel: Why do you think?
> Adrienne: OMG . . . are you the boss?
> Jamiel: What's OMG? And, yes I am.

It finally made sense why his bizarre behaviour was so overlooked easily by the rest of the staff. OMG, I hope the boss likes me.

A few days later and I had to ask Jamiel again about my dad on the way home.

'I have been waiting for you to ask' was his annoying response.

'Can you just tell me how you know my dad and what else do you know about him?'

'I only know what I have been able to mathematically reconstruct.'

'What the hell does that even mean?'

'You are a really smart, young woman for a normal human' was his response. I wasn't sure whether I was complimented or insulted. He'd done that before.

'Okay' he broke the silence. 'I'll tell you what I mean. Why does your mum need you home so quickly after work? Where does she go as soon as you are home to mind your baby brother while she disappears until the next morning? How do you live in such a home that you told me your mother owns outright when she has no job? Why does your home have gates so far away from the front door when no other house in this half of Sydney can afford a decent front door? Why do you think that both your father as well as your baby brother's father come nowhere near either of you, your mother, or the house?

'Over the years, Rennie, I have learned to rebuild human behaviour based upon the way people dress, walk, speak, what they own, and how they decide to disclose information. I often get it wrong, but the parts that can be drawn with maths can be seen by me better than most. I'm sure of it.'

I knew it could be all explained by my mother's simple story that I've known all my life.

'Jamiel, my mum was treated very badly by my dad and so he had to go and has never come back, not even to wish me a happy birthday.' I'm not sure that he could read the level of distress on my face, and so he continued on just before we arrived outside my place with the following very calm statement:

'Your description is inconsistent with two things. One, your mother has no issue screaming at you in front of me, and I'm not a small male. Two, you're really short and your mother is not, so your father is likely really short. So why would your mother fear a man smaller than a man she doesn't fear—being me?'

'Yes, Jamiel, I get that you meant you.' No one had ever forced me to confront these points put forward by Jamiel in his typically logical fashion. I wanted to know more, but he would only say the following: 'You need to discover these points for yourself.'

'How?' I asked as he murmured a 'geez' with limited facial expression.

'Imagine being back at school, and that this is a project. You'll figure it out, smart woman for a human.'

'By the way,' he told me as he was driving off, 'I know what OMG means.'

So without boring you with the following few weeks of investigating, it turns out that Jamiel was right and I had come to not be surprised. I was looking forward to telling him at work the next day, but forgot to get to it when I saw cars being towed out of our showroom. Jamiel was standing at the mezzanine, with his usual blank face.

'Do I still have a job?' was my first thought, but what I let out to Jamiel was, 'What happened to all the vroom vroom?'

He kept staring into space whilst saying, 'The house I built to help others was a house of cards that others have now knocked down.'

'C'mon Jamiel,' I replied to a man that probably wasn't listening, 'You still have your financial firm.' I was waiting to be replied to with what I had now come to expect would be something no one else would

say in that situation and I was not disappointed. 'Rennie, a house of
cards doesn't look like it's falling when you are in it, until the final
crash.'

'Ah, okay' was now my usual reply when I had no idea what he was
saying.

'I have absolutely no idea why this is happening, but my lawyer says
I am autistic.'

'You're not retarded, Jamiel, if that is what autistic means. You're
just weird.'

His voice was fading even further as fewer cars remained in the
showroom. 'I should never have learned from Sabrina how to look more
human. I should never have survived the suicide.'

Not even my ray of sunshine could brighten up the mountain's day.

'Sorry, Jamiel, I have no joke to make you feel better.'

His reply shot out very quickly. 'Rennie . . . I thought I survived my
past for a reason . . . to help others, to change the world, but all that has
happened is a nightmare from which I don't think my future self will
escape, and I still don't know why this is happening.'

I really wished he wasn't speaking to me in riddles at that point, but
I had known him long enough to know he already had a plan for me.

'There is a man whose life I once saved. He is going to call you and
offer you a job. It's not a good job, nor a well-paying one, but you need
to prove to both me and yourself that you really want to be as successful
as you say you do before I can help you get there.'

Rennie's escape

My mum asked me where I was going when I was dressed in my
black shirt and pants as requested by the new job I had as a waitress.
There was no way I was coming back home if I was leaving to work as
a waitress, according to the woman that looked like me as she towered
over me with that face I had grown to fear.

I knew I had to stand up to my mother for the first time in my life,
and so I packed a bag and disappeared out the door.

Jamiel was right as I hated the job but would stick to it and not go
home to a woman that forbade me to leave the house. It was Sabrina's
turn to rescue me with a safe place to stay that evening whilst I heard her

professionally defending my right to work against a psychotic mother. I could hear her through the phone, two rooms away. Whatever was said to Sabrina gave her the face of someone who had glimpsed horror.

'I have to take you home' was all she said in a robotic voice.

Sabrina was a very strong and very smart woman and was my role model. Now she was even scared of my mum. I cried as Mum made me give her my phone, wallet, passport, money, and laptop before locking me in my room.

The wind outside was especially intrusive. It almost sounded like it was speaking.

'Hey,' it said. 'HEY,' it said again. It reminded me of Jamiel.

'Rennie!' It was Jamiel whispering only a metre away from me from outside my window.

'Jamiel! Oh my god . . . what the hell are you doing here?'

'Be quiet,' he whispered, 'take this phone and set your old phone to visible so I can track it with my iPad. Sabrina told me about how your mum threatened to harm her parents. Your mum is evil, and I will get you away from here soon and to your true family.'

'Why are you risking yourself to help me?' was my question to my old boss, hoping to hear an inspiring reply.

'I would do this for anyone,' he answered, 'and it gives me a reason to keep going.' With that, he disappeared into the shadows.

I snuck into Mum's empty room and set my old phone to visible as Jamiel had requested. I now knew I would be safe.

Mum found my back-up phone and was infuriated as I had never before witnessed; the walls were trembling before her voice. I was, in fact, so scared that I told the police—whom Jamiel had sent to Mum's house after not hearing from me for two days—that there was no problem and that Jamiel was over-reacting. The police stated that they would tell Jamiel to leave us alone. I am sure that Jamiel would take their request literally and give up on helping me. After managing to get hold of a phone that belonged to a friend visiting Mum a few days later, I discovered that he had. I begged him to help me but not to reply to any texts. Other than that, I would simply have to wait until a chance came again to contact him.

When it came again, I told him that I was too scared to leave the house and would wait for Mum to calm down enough to let me out of the house again. Jamiel was enraged. 'Are you insane? My brother Micah, my best friend Eleina, and I have been working on a comprehensive plan to get you away to a safe location with the help of the Australian government. We did not do all this work so that the human that spat you out of her womb could lock you and your future away from this country.'

I hurled out a laugh so loud at the weird sentence I should not have been surprised hearing.

'Why are you laughing, Rennie? We have limited time and you are choosing to fill it with laughter?'

I couldn't stop despite knowing that by 'the Australian government' he must have meant some social service funded by the government.

'Rennie, you can stay imprisoned if that is what you wish, but let me know now so that we know what we need to do.'

I would do it. I would give up everything I knew for a life I had no idea would be better or worse. Jamiel said that 'your mother's personality is consistent with one that may use your love for your baby brother against you, so remember that if you say bye to him it will be for a very long time if not forever.'

Seconds passed before I heard Jamiel say to Eleina and Micah, 'She's not answering. What do I do?'

I heard what must have been Eleina's voice yelling at Jamiel to 'just stay on the line until she was ready to speak'.

I leaned over my baby brother's sleeping face and kissed him goodbye as my warm tears flowed over his glistening skin and sheets glowing from the moonlight. After what felt like a very long time, I picked up the phone and asked Jamiel if he was still there.

'She's back, Eleina,' I heard Jamiel say followed by a 'Yes, I'm still here.'

'If I describe a place to you that is special to me, can you be there in forty-five minutes?'

'Describe the place and I'll tell you how long it will take me to get there.'

I waited near the statue until I saw the large man in the distance. 'Rennie,' his voiced boomed out through the cold night and past the statue I had been hiding behind for the past hour.

I walked towards the man with caution until I knew for sure that it was Jamiel. As soon as I knew it was him, I ran towards him. Whether it was out of fear or relief, I'm not sure, but I ran straight into his arms as he consoled me with 'You are safe now. Let's get you out of here.'

I jumped into his dad's car before we began our trip out of Sydney.

'Rennie. Listen carefully as I will not be with you for a while. Don't be scared, as you will be safe with the division of the government to which I am sending you. They will not divulge your whereabouts to anyone including me, so you must remain courageous in your decision to throw away your prison for freedom.'

'Where are you taking me now if you cannot know where I am going?'

'Well Rennie, Eleina, Micah, and I have been able to find you a safe place to stay for the evening before Sabrina can get you a small car to drive to a location where a social services employee will take you to a safe house. But as soon as I get you to your temporary safe house for the evening, you will need to call the police on this number and let them know that you are okay and have ran away from your mother. At least that way they can be shown that I was not wrong in pleading with them to go to your place that time when you made me look like the bad guy.'

'How are you not scared of my mum in doing all this, Jamiel? You know that she has connections to the wrong kinds of people, right?' Nothing phased this man still with his limited facial expressions.

'Rennie, your mother has already had men call and threaten me and my family, as well as sending her toupee-wearing, married boyfriend to Sabrina's brother. I have been to the police who have now told me multiple times that there is nothing they can do until your birth mother strikes, but the best thing to do with this type of person is to drag them out into the light. This is why you need to strengthen yourself, write down your story, and then share it with the police as soon as you are safely out of Sydney.

'Anyway, we have a long drive ahead of us so how about I tell you a true story about a kid that almost everyone thought was mentally disabled, who was abused, harassed, bashed, arrested as a Jewish spy in Syria, who fell off a cliff, who survived a suicide-induced coma, only to discover that he was some sort of genius who built an empire with the hope of saving the world before it collapsed in a heap.'

'Are you talking about yourself, Jamiel?'

'Yes, Rennie. Yes I am.'

'Okay! Let's do this.'

SPEAKING HUMAN
Volume 1: The tragedy of the retarded genius

My gift is a curse

'Adrienne, it took almost three decades to be accepted as human by the average family and through helping them, I was able to then help many others—funding hundreds of surgeries in countries I'd never visited. This was what life was for, and together we would change the world for the better.'

That was the dream, and this story is the tragedy.

'So how did you meet Eleina?'

Eleina was assigned to represent an individual that had decided to make me their enemy for their own personal gain. Unlike those around her, she saw through the steel wall of cynicism built to save those in power from having to think more about what may seem an open-shut case.

'I'm guessing you won't be telling me what that means in English, Jamiel?'

I thought it would be best to share with Adrienne some words I could recall directly from Eleina:

Watching them all; his staff, comprised of the standard human, continued providing him with social interaction he would continue to memorise. Only thinking that 'his gift truly was a curse' was the lens from which he would watch the house of cards fall; as the coma from whence his hope to change the world was born was now only the beginning of a story of tragedy.

He needed to help others, he was chosen—that had to have been why he survived the suicide against the odds of severe damage his mind should have suffered. Rather, he discovered his brain could see dimensions that to all others did not exist at all.

He found it illogical when his staff seemed to interact with whom they found likeable, completely disregarding one's putrid character through contradictions of their behaviour over time.

This, as we know, is what one would expect as a neurotypical human being. He had learned to mask himself as one, but still understood them naught.

They would misjudge him as did the world before his failed suicide, as all the world would do after it.

The above sounded very depressing to Adrienne which in no way was my intention, so I thought I'd share more about Eleina's opinion of the man others call Jamiel who only months before had been in rebel-occupied Syria enjoying a sandwich and western-style coffee.

Eleina's confusion

I still don't know what to make of the contradiction.

I saw him make out the Cyrillic alphabet in less than five minutes and heard the native accent that shortly followed. The second time I ran in to him, he was speaking to me in Hebrew which I am sure he didn't know only weeks before, and yet despite all this, he was convinced he was an idiot.

I couldn't say whether he had no self-esteem, or no concept of self-esteem at all.

Wandering into the courts, he would simply commence legal proceedings against companies that had wronged him, innocently demolishing their legal representatives by just replying to each argument with a coherent response; or 'not getting bogged down with deviations from the logic axis' as he would say; yet he seemed to have no idea that this was so rare.

Always wondering why human actions seemed so illogical to him, he observed them with the hope of becoming one of them; putting them first and himself nowhere—eventually, and inevitably, falling into harm's way. It was only a matter of time before he would be famous, and for all the wrong reasons.

I am certain that he is not understood. Like a child never beaten into conforming to society, he was what I'd consider to be a real human; something for the rest of us to aspire to. Don't ask him to believe anything but the exact opposite, but nevertheless, I felt normal around him, and I loved him for that. I wouldn't admit that I still did, though . . . if I did.'

'So Eleina likes you, Jamz!'

I had to reply to the accurate statement:
'Of course she likes me. If she didn't like me, she wouldn't be my friend and fight for the unlikely version of events instead of the likely. This is the only logical move when dealing with a person who is himself an unlikely form of human.'

It turns out that that wasn't what Adrienne had meant, but if it kept the young lady away from thoughts of her sociopathic mother then I was happy to humour her.

'So what else did Eleina notice about you that you didn't know about your weird self, tall boy?'

I gave her a small list: via a question I once asked Eleina:

'How can I, Eleina,

keep pretending I am of your species when I am reminded
that I am not with every second that passes?
Before you, I had no idea
that people could walk down a street and
be clueless about how many cars passed by them on one side,
vs the number of shops they had passed on the other.
They don't even remember how many conversations they had passed,
what was said,
and in what language.
Yet I am forced to live here as though I was one of them.'

'Okay, Mr Memory', giggled out from Adrienne's mouth, 'how many restaurants have we passed?'

'Sixteen, where three of them had four wheel drives in their respective car parks while two others had only one family each that were viewable from outside the restaurants as we were driving past. The last one was a little hard to see since it is only now twelve kilometres behind us and the sun was setting at that time. The main problem is that I could be wrong about anything or everything I've just said and we would never know unless we drove back to check all sixteen restaurants, which also happens to be four more than the number of timber pieces on the back wall of a Thai restaurant in Dulwich hill.'

Despite the chance I was completely wrong, Adrienne was still excited with the reply. I still find this type of reaction from people to be completely weird.

'Anyway, Rennie, may I get on with the story, or is it boring you?'
'C'mon Jamiel, get on with the story. I wanna know more!'

'Okay, but the jigsaw is not complete and is sandwiched throughout by comments on the past by an older me who could since articulate what the younger, autistic Jamiel could not. I wish you well with it, and smile at the thought of you making sense of this strange life that may help you relate to the strangeness of others.'

'You're the only strange person I know so far, Jamiel'

PROLOGUE

MEMORY

For whatever reason, the younger me had the need to imitate the behaviour of men, appearing to do it naturally. The irony would come years later, when the illusion of normality would allow me to suffer consequences from which an obviously atypical human mind would have been exempt.

Before learning to control them, my memories would swim and scream whenever consciousness was around. The sounds of life would do nothing but tickle my brain into dropping memories into an already flooded space behind my eyeballs; so loud that focusing on anything was a laughable proposition. Like branches from a single tree spreading into a forest—a piece of music, a conversation snatch, the noise of a particular engine, a certain smell, a colour, a set of numbers— anything at all, stimulated a rush of memories that fed into a violent waterfall of others and others.

The memories were vivid and never faded with time. As though happening only yesterday, the concept of memory as related to time had been foreign for two and a half decades. How the few people I had encountered long enough to witness them 'get over' something since it was 'in the past' was a fantastic notion. Nothing was in the 'past'; since if it had occurred, it was as real on the day of revisiting as it was when it happened.

Becoming, to some degree, a functioning adult has been attained in part through revisiting those same memories with an older mind and a lot of help; and while they fade at the slowest of paces, I can clearly see the person from which I have evolved. The videos are still there to tell the story as it was—and today I tell it you.

PART 1

Numbers are just letters in a story for me.
1993 was the year I first realised I could end all the misery. That year would have been at least the equivalent of six years for an adult.

North East Boys Private College brought with it a new sense of worthlessness. Growing up with limited interaction with people outside of the working class family brought with it no readiness to deal with students arriving to school in shiny, late-model automobiles with hair that somehow remained wet throughout the day, and drawing both teachers and other students to them with a force I could not detect.

The other 'F#####g Lebos', as one teacher referred to them, weren't comfortable with this tall and awkward Semitic male who claimed to be of Maronite descent while using 'funny English words' when not speaking their language as an attempt to prove the claim.

Reaching puberty at age 9 brought with it hairs in strange places that saw one of the boys commenting to the rest with unusual interest during gym class.

I suppose that we looked like penguins in our school uniforms, with daily inspections ensuring our legs were covered by the long socks to the knee. I can now articulate the shear fear of the possibility of failing this test on a daily basis. Some students would drop their socks as soon as they were off school property, but with some students reporting back to the year master I was too scared to do this—having learned from the man called my father, that I must be immaculate and perfect in appearance.

Guys were using pens at this school. They were so inconsiderate in leaving those pens facing me with their lids off. Images of exposed pens all around the room would burrow deep into my skin, not getting any quieter throughout the day. It didn't seem that anyone had a problem with turning 180 degrees without turning back to avoid getting tangled up in the cords created by their compulsions. Perhaps they had learned to handle the task more fluently. However they achieved it, I began to hear increasing heckling of other kids occurring more frequently around the yard.

I was starting to think the heckling might have been aimed at me, but Mum explained that I may have just been overthinking it. To test the hypothesis, I decided to force my behaviour away from its instinctive patterns, such as avoiding the stepping on of cracks. This was easy outside of school, where riding my bike as much as possible kept the cracks away from my feet and the loudness of the day's memories from my ears.

'Jason,' my watch mailed to me from the Mediterranean as a gift at age 10 by uncle. 'Pretty boy' Henry, whom I'd met when I was 6 in the green mountains of Dad's childhood home, was a square-faced and quiet timekeeper. Mum explained that the gift belonged on the left wrist, so I kept him there. It was fascinating to see the numbers change constantly on Jason's face. He was predictable and made sense, and played no games when sharing the sequence of numbers which were divisible by so many smaller ones. This was the only way to simplify all my activities by mentally recording how long each would take as a percentage of the day.

From the first day at North East, my little version became obsessed with synchronising Jason with the school bell. The seconds running down to the screaming of the bell would instigate both happiness and anxiety within me depending on what time of day it was ringing. Jason wouldn't hide the time from me regardless.

Every minute, and every second was precious; how many minutes were in the lesson and how many seconds that was; whether one lesson was longer than the other; how long was our last break and how many minutes between breaks; how long it would take to get from the class to where I would eat my lunch so I knew how much time I would have to deduct from my lunch hour and how long it would take to eat my lunch.

This knowledge made me feel quite powerful and I thought it would make the other kids want to be friends with me; I would tell them that the bell would be going off in the exact number of minutes and seconds.

They didn't seem that interested; however, they did like to remind me that I was first one in and the first one out of the classroom.

Handball was a task I was strangely good at, and beating the wet-haired big boys during lunch hour raised my adrenalin levels to new heights, at which point it would seem that my mind ticked faster than usual, thereby slowing down the speed of the match. This form of time dilation was the extra edge needed to topple the would-be handball champions of the grade. Stronger players would bizarrely form alliances with weaker ones. I found this unbelievably strange but found their reactions even stranger as I'd take out these weak links piece by piece. The fear of their reactions against me combined with the exhilaration of conquering the popular in the hope of capturing some of that popularity made the whole hour travel much more quickly.

The obvious contradiction between the two time flows made it abundantly clear that the uniform flow of time had to be an illusion. How could this not be brought up with the guys? But unfortunately when discussing this apparent contradiction in the flow of time, I was looked at, generally with confusion. *'I must be making this stuff up'* I thought. *'It is not possible that not one other student gets what I am saying'*

In control of time, but not yet of making friends.

I won a digital stopwatch from an MS read-athon I'd entered. He was unreliable by going out of sync on a daily basis which was unacceptable from something claiming to be a watch. I didn't join many read-athons after that and prayed that I wouldn't get MS because of this.

'So you were religious back then, Jamiel?'

Anyway. . .

Every week, Jason would be out by a second or two each time and I would calculate how many seconds we were losing a month. I'd reset him every week and after a while he got pretty good at staying in sync for quite a while, with my regular 'Jason adjustments'.

One teacher in particular used to ask me the time over and over.
'What's the time Jamie?'
'One seventeen and ten seconds.'
'What's the time Jamie?'
'One seventeen and thirteen seconds.'

He just kept asking me and I just kept answering. I initially assumed this was a great man who understood the concept of truly knowing the time; however, after a while, I noticed that this didn't seem consistent with the fact that he was a moron.

I really didn't see how this was funny.

This had to be a prank by my parents. There was no reason I could see that I would be fair game for abuse by teachers and other kids. I had answers for most questions asked, and knew stuff that other kids, and even teachers, didn't know. Except for Alex "general knowledge" McDoogal, who was brilliant at getting knowledge out at seemingly the right time, my mouth was the first to open with an answer or my hand the first one to go up.

One teacher telling me that there was no such word as 'prequel' was one such example of the above. I remember this being in 1992 and I also remember that I unfortunately argued back as I was rightfully convinced that he was incorrect, but wrongly convinced that this would matter to him.

Other teachers would ask me to leave the room and then walk back in and say 'hello' with**out** yelling. I would do this, only to get asked to do it again, but this time with**out** yelling.

I was punished for what was normal for me. So I began to think I was not only a loud-mouthed trouble-maker, but also an idiot. There was no question that there was *something wrong with me* compared to these people, and I wanted out.

A teacher would ask us to read a book for homework. I couldn't understand why they were making fun of me when I had finished the book by the next day whilst they were still stuck on the first chapter. I really thought they had all finished the book but were pretending to be on the first chapter to make fun of me. This had to be the reason. It wasn't possible that they could have only read a few pages.

My mother read to us until I was three, when I took over reading to myself and left my brother to eventually grow tired of reading completely. I could not stop reading from that point on. I read novel after novel in my mother's beautiful library of books until the age of 6, when I then turned to reading nonfiction; such as the dictionary, scientific journals, and the history of Greek mythology. I was proud of myself in 1988 at age 7, when I read a document as fast as my Mum did. There was no reason to believe that the other kids didn't have the same experiences I did, and I assumed this was what people did when they were 'reading'.

1991 was the year of the disastrous teacher called Mr Stuart. He was much younger than my parents and wore a blonde mullet; looking like the type of guy from a 1980s TV beer ad. He made malicious remarks about me in front of the class and this encouraged the class to join in. He would yell at me in front of everyone. He made fun of my hand writing, which was pretty bad, but he behaved as if I was doing it deliberately (I discovered this word in 1989 from the back of a liquid paper bottle that Jonathon had smuggled into class at St John's). Mr Stuart said I didn't show initiative.

Once he made me stand with my arms in the air for forty-five minutes in front of the class because I defended someone else he made fun of. Everything Mr Stuart said would trigger a question and my hand would go up, but I had too many questions. Once I had my hand up for nine minutes and thirty-nine seconds (I think) but it wasn't working. Maybe I wasn't doing it right.

By the end of Year 6, my academic standard had begun to decline and this was quite odd because all through primary school, attention was constantly drawn to the fact that I would be the one guy getting better marks than the girls. I then deduced that the guys must now be performing much better that there were no girls in the class and had left me behind. In Year 7, they even put me in the D Maths class—D Maths! Considering I had been recording the patterns I made from tossing coins and finding a 'number' relationship between my old baby bike and the BMX with a chain at the age of six, I now began to doubt myself. My head was full of negative thoughts. I must have been dumb.

28.10.2013
'Dad! I'm teaching a French class today!'
'How ken u tich afrrrensh wen u cant spik it?'

My conscious mind would often break out of the present moment as it jumped into one of the many open windows to other worlds awaiting it. Before long, the classroom noise was nowhere to be heard.

'What do you think, Jamiel?' I remember hearing after being spewed back into reality.

'Where am I . . . ah, yes. . .' I thought to myself, 'they want to talk to me. Hold on,' I then thought, 'what are they talking about again?'

'Are you here, Jamiel?' would be the next question from the teacher with some students shaking their heads.

Anxiety was here, although the younger me could not describe the reaction that was leaving his skin sweaty and his breathing heavily. The dream of being contacted by fellow humans was here. I needed it. Please don't leave my grasp.

'Sorry, sir, what was the question again?'

I knew the attacks would be coming at the end of class: 'You just love the attention, don't you, Levant?'

'No, you fool, whom I wish would be my friend,' hoping he couldn't read my mind, 'and I really didn't hear what the teacher said,' I would be desperate to say.

Why couldn't I respond, and better yet, why in the name of all things decent did I keep tuning out?

Massive effort was required to get up each day to go to school, but wondering if it could ever get worse was a mistake, as that was before . . . high school.

Enter Year 7, and my English teacher was Mr Summers, an authoritative man in his late thirties with black, tight curly hair who wore smart suits in odd colours. Perhaps younger me was mistaken, but he seemed to enjoy knowing everything and wanted to espouse a one-way theory upon it. This meant that on the receiving end of his thoughts was a 'no entry sign' for feedback. Of course this was only discovered by me after traversing that path, wondering why not many others would question what needed to be examined. I truly believed I was helping him when correcting his factually mistaken comments.

And kids found some of my remarks funny and laughed and that made me feel good for a minute, not getting why they were laughing, but enjoying the visiting of attention before its impending departure. Some remarks didn't get a response, so obviously I would have to state them with a raised voice to ensure that I'd helped Mr Summers for the day.

One day, Mr Summers asked the class, 'Put your hand up if you think Jamiel is funny.'

After looking around the room at each other, two kids put their hands up. He then said, 'Put your hand up if you think Jamiel is an idiot.'

It seemed that a sea of hands was reaching for the ceiling.

He sat perched on the corner of his desk, watching and smiling. I smiled too as I turned and saw my classmates with their hands up. Some apologised for doing so later on which I found, yet again, bizarre. Why do it in the first place if that was the case . . . but ultimately, I concluded that I must have been an idiot. It had been statistically proven beyond doubt. Sometime after that incident, Mr Summers called me into his office. I was excited; perhaps he would finally reward me in secret for helping him all this time.

He conveniently sat me down on a chair that was lower than his and looked down at me with what seemed to me be a smiling face, but quickly changing to a face with an expression I could not understand. In a low voice he began, 'You are trouble; you disrupt the class. . .' His eyes were piercing and his voice was getting louder and louder. *'You are a rude boy!'*

'Ah, now I understand the face he was making. He wants to kill me,' I surmised.

With absolutely no idea why he was screaming at me, the younger me tried desperately to focus before Mr Summers' face began to take up all of the view, and as a consequence of this, little Jamiel would lose perspective and rapidly all feeling in his rapidly growing body. Later on in the day, I was told that Mr Summers' screaming could be heard from the next building across the street dividing the lower and upper school grades.

After the damning exposure of me as an idiot, I decided it was smart to get in with that fact before kids started abusing me. Walking past almost any other student, I would save hearing their judgements upon me by jumping in first: 'Guess what,' I said with a smile each time, 'Jamiel's an idiot.'

At least I learned a new facial expression that day.

The Death of Nansia the first
The discovery of Nansia the second

No one survived the Middle Eastern Airlines flight that exploded over the border of Jordan and Kuwait on its way back to Australia on January 1 of 1976, including my father's big sister, Nansia, along with her husband and two young sons. My father was at the airport, waiting for them to arrive home. He would come back to the airport every day for a further two weeks, waiting for them to come out of the airport doors; all the while knowing their remains were now scattered over foreign sands.

Before that fateful day, he had discovered Mum. Not only with the same name as big sis, but a small, pale olive-skinned, super strong personality with red curls that would bounce as she walked past him with piercing green eyes, giving him no second thought as she carried her books home. It was a year before he spoke to her, but through the Maronite community was able to find out enough about her to be head over heels. A qualified private detective, he read newspapers at conveniently placed park benches; not to stalk her, as he swears, but as her 'protector'.

Mum's dad couldn't help but speak little and had even less interest in people but could remember every card that had passed his eyes in a card game, and in which order. Renowned for this, Dad (the buffed up 'Christopher Reeve' look-alike in his early twenties) learned to play enough to be punished severely by Grandad on an almost daily basis; anything to see his future bride. With even looks such as that in a community where such a look was in no way the stereotype, my mother would ignore him with ease; desiring a career before any man . . . until the day he really pissed her off. He had just arrived from a funeral and looked to Mum like a typical conformist:

'Why are you wearing a black tie? It looks stupid.'

Finally! She had spoken to him.

He promptly requested a pair of scissors and cut right through the only tie he had.

'Forrr yoo, I will nevrr weyrr black tie agenn.'

They were married in 1977.

Changing Australia
A child mute

Twentieth-century Lebanon was a French formed, Maronite-Catholic-driven society that, in all fairness, treated neither its growing Islamic population nor its other Christian populations as perfect equals. This breeding ground for anti-Western sentiment helped fertilise the subsequent civil war which then trickled down into a 1970s deal between a new Australian government and some oil-producing nations in the Middle East, bringing forth a new wave of Lebanese and Palestinian immigrants to Sydney. This time they were of an Arabic/Islamic culture, with starkly contrasting views with the established Maronite populations too often leading to undesirable clashes, ultimately changing the cultural mix of Lakemba, and just like in their old homeland, a slow move out by Maronites.

Mum's family wasn't so easily disturbed, leaving Mum and Dad to shift only to the neighbouring working class suburb of Greenacre; some seventeen kilometres south west of Sydney's heart.

Tiny Nansia suffered a difficult birth at 7.30 a.m. on Friday the thirteenth of February launching forth a child at almost 10 per cent of her total body mass. This child would not stop crying, giving her and her loving husband no sleep, yet she remained diligent with almost encyclopaedic records of her son's babyhood. I saw his baby blonde hair again twenty-nine years later. This child did not speak for over two years, learning to play a colour-coded keyboard from a correspondingly coded music sheet before this time, as well as witnessing the presence of a much quieter younger brother.

Family's worries over the mute child increased until the day he bypassed single words, jumping straight into whole sentences in 1983 in both Maronite-Arabic and English. From that point on, I didn't stop.

THE GREAT LIONS, AND THE
FOREST BEFORE THE POOL

There's no 'empty space' in my head. I used to ask people what they were thinking and wonder how they could think 'nothing' when my head pulsating like a neutron star; banging with colours, sounds, images, videos, scents from memories, and their associated feelings of embarrassment, sadness, anger, and sometimes even joy.

'You should look at a particular subject from a "different perspective",' once explained a primary school teacher. Mum explained this to mean looking at something from a different angle. Lying awake until the early hours of the morning, I would wonder what the past day would have looked like from a different physical viewpoint. 'Perhaps I just constantly witness the day's events from the wrong position in the classroom,' I would think for many years to come.

Apart from one disputed memory at the age of ten months, vivid memories from my 2-year-old self lie deep within me, like Mum taking me and brother Micah to the health care centre, where the nurse put him in a cradle on the scales with me saying, 'I used to be weighed in there.' I asked if I could be weighed again, with the Brady Bunch housekeeper look-alike saying 'You're a bit too big now.' Mum wrote words on flash cards like 'parentheses' and 'annunciate' for me to recite, and then to put together using the provided alphabet blocks.

Toys were educational and I loved them, especially any that involved my native language of numbers.

Preschool at age 3 saw the inception of not fitting in. My mother was called in to be told that her child possessed 'social difficulties'. One wise teacher who understood me was great to talk to, unintentionally helping me keep up the illusion that I was the normal kid.

The back fence of the preschool was where mini-me found peace away from the yelling masses. I would stand, and never sit, on the grass, peering through the fence and to the thin blue line of the local swimming pool's surface. Imagine walking along the pathway to the pool through the forest of beautiful large trees past the two large lions of concrete that never faltered in their stance, signifying the entrance to the 'forest before the pool'; the quiet border town between school kids and adults. Autumn days were when the wind and sky between the trees would be mixed with the brown of the circling leaves. The leaves danced with the wind, and I would dance with them.

The sun streamed through these onto the vividly green grass like a scene out of C.S Lewis' Narnia. Sometime later, the teachers banned that location, along with the rolling of the car tyre which other kids would 'brilliantly' roll into each other's way. The hallucinations started at age four. 'Can't you hear them, Mum?' She would reply . . . and I would say, 'I can't hear you; I can hear them.' The holographic giants would stomp past the child like an earth-quaking foot patrol. I kept asking Mum to make them go away, with her trying to calm me down with a cloth soaked in vinegar and cold water to the forehead. The army would not return as the child grew, but beyond the vinegar, this was never addressed.

Mum dragged a teary-eyed Dad away from his traumatised son at his first day of school. It took all of her strength to keep her husband from running back to the crying child who was begging to know why he was being abandoned. I sat away from others as much as I could, focusing on the analogue clock on the classroom wall, calculating how long it would be in hours and minutes before 'Mum would be coming to pick me up'.

Mousy brown-haired Miss Kara would permit me exceptions that I would unconsciously begin to expect from all future dealings with authority. She let me alone in the classroom during lunch hour, where I would recreate the suburb of Greenacre between school and home with hundreds of wooden cubes. The child was obsessed with how many roads there were between home and school and where each intersected with another, as well as scrutinising our surrounding suburbs via the street directory. The compulsion to break the sticks in two almost had me banned from building the roads, but just almost.

Ultimately, nothing overrode the obsession with time. Trying to cut a slab of cold, white chocolate with the largest kitchen knife available saw me slicing my left index finger open at 6.28 p.m. on Sunday, October 10, 1989—courtesy of the gold hexagonal-shaped clock on the kitchen wall. The rich, red blood spurt over the white chocolate two minutes before a concert I didn't attend, and one week before my first holy communion. Two years later, my mum asked Micah, 'So Jamie played the piano at his holy communion. What are you going to play at yours?'

'The computer,' he answered.

Playing outside was when I would witness the most bizarre of behaviour, where kids did stupid things together and laughed at things that could not possibly have been funny. Like one girl with short and blonde curly hair yelling, 'I can see your undies. You've got red undies,' she squealed, laughing, and spreading the word.

I didn't find that funny, but it was definitely hilarious when a cousin got punched in the face by a volleyball (that was so funny) whilst receiving stares of death for laughing. One kid asked if I was 'horny' in 1987 to which of course I replied 'yes'. The kids laughed and I thought, 'Cool, I'm horny.' That night after giving the good news to Mum, she sat me down and explained a few things.

Almost blinded on a daily basis by overwhelming external stimuli, the last thing I needed was to be touched. I f*** hated it, and would be socially smashed for blowing the burning touch of other school kids off me always. I did, however, want their friendship, and would watch while it would slip from my grasp on a daily basis. Two boys decided to talk to me: David and Jonathan. I truly appreciated that.

Kids would make friends by bringing toys to school. There was no logic in this, but after having this concept rubbed in my face for so long, it had to be tried. This strategy was finally attempted by bringing in my new set of crayons, and although the kids took the crayons, used them, broke them and didn't bring them back, I had attention . . . and it was awesome.

Where the sun set over the sea

Dad entered the world via a green valley furnished with serene beauty, protected by gigantic snowy peaks, and a narrow, misty view of the light blue Mediterranean. His mother was warned repeatedly that she would die if she allowed Dad to be born, but was filled with too much love to act otherwise.

The death of Dad's mother shortly after his birth would make him the youngest of seven children.

His father, a man who had spent his young life in the military, felt it would be best to disperse his four boys and three girls, amongst his closest relatives, with the eldest boy named 'Just' passing away of an unknown illness not long thereafter.

Catholic boarding school in North Lebanon looked after Dad when he was old enough, but unlike Mum, young Father was not as academically inclined, spending his summer vacations in the cool mountainous regions of his home, applying himself to enormous physical work and spending his nights with his friends in the village.

While most of us are quite tall, he was short and stocky but physically strong. He would work on the olive press, pushing around the massive wheel to grind out oil, and was eventually replaced with a horse.

His homesickness finally convinced Mum to bring all four of us on the journey that his big sister's family of four never made back. By now my brother and I were aged six and four, and were the same age as our two late cousins when they were blown to pieces. From Cyprus I was introduced to the vile effects of sea-sickness, before bypassing the sectarian war in Beirut to dock at the Maronite stronghold of Junieh.

It was weird to finally be sitting in the driver's seat only to witness the steering wheel stuck to the wrong side of the dash. The weather was perfect in the upper atmosphere of the alpine towns just below the melting snow, leaving me in a perpetual state of excitement. Hearing people utter strange words with strange accents, I could not stop asking anyone who would listen to explain what any word meant. Pattern forming was focused solely on this mutated language I had to master.

Kids swinging from the ropes over mountain rivers, bathed in warm sunlight while the adults enjoyed picnics with such animated body language were intense memories that kept a warm glow long after the mountains were far away.

Easter was televised as widely as a viral video; people out of their homes, candles everywhere, food in abundance, and the illusion of family and happiness left me with great feelings of attachment to this strange place where the sun set over the sea.

I was greeted with addictive attention upon my return to school. Kids seemed especially interested in the shooting in the neck I had witnessed only a few metres away during some inter-Christian scuffle.

One of the teachers got a new boy who had just arrived from Lebanon to sit next to me so I could teach him English, but when I started explaining things to him, the teacher asked me to stop talking. I thought that was odd.

Between ages 9 and 6, and expressions.

Garry invited me to his place to play after school but kept running from room to room as I would approach. Curiosity forced me to follow him and his friends to each room and wait at the door until they decided to run to the next location, allowing myself to enjoy observing how they behaved with each other whilst they spoke in 'code' until Garry came up to me and said I was a loser, and to go and play by myself in his room.

Pretending to have understood the 'code', I stood before Garry until he said it again and laughed whilst walking back to his followers. Maybe this was a setup, and I was now stuck there. The weight of tears came to my eyes and I did not want anyone to see. Unfortunately, Emma did see and immediately told Garry's mum. Gary was then forced to allow me in to his cult. They were really nice to me after that, so I decided that maybe all the other kids had already been through this with Garry's mum individually prior to me meeting them. I suspected, years later, that Mum had asked Garry's mother to invite me; she denied this.

I didn't think asking people over to my house would be a good idea. I was imagining Dad switching between asking questions about their families and constantly presenting them with food. I invited a kid with the same name as my baby brother, Micah, to my eighth birthday party and gave him my phone number for him to RSVP. Later that evening, I was listening to the messages on our answering machine with Mum and heard something quite strange: 'Hi, this is Micah and you're an idiot.' My mum later heard it a few times and stated, 'That is not what he said. It just sounds like that'. 'I will go talk to him to find out what he actually said. Don't worry, I am certain he is sending you well wishes.'

My mum was right, it seems, as Micah was so nice to me from the next day onwards at school.

There were too many people around in the McDonalds where I had my eighth birthday, and I could feel them all laughing at me whilst I retreated to underneath the table. Reaching up for the ice cream cake, I successfully landed it on my face. Mum tried to lovingly get me back up with the group by letting me know I was a sook. At least the kids were entertained.

Did things sound the same to each human, or did they differ with each person?

'Mum, do you think vegemite tastes the same to each person, or does it taste to me like spaghetti tastes to you?' I could come up with no theory at the time to explain why not one relative living in those mountains tolerated vegemite in the slightest.

Imagine being a grown adult and forced to sit through primary school where the teacher assumes you can read only picture books, and then forces you to endure the torture of kids trying to unsuccessfully put this into action. Do you feel that frustration? How many days of this would you sit through before heading straight over heals into madness . . . I'd love to know.

Miss Jenny in Year 1 was good to me; she was short and round with freckles, and gave me extra work to do on my own. Like others, she would constantly ask me to not be so loud, but unlike others she smiled when asking. In contrast, Miss Sandra in Year 2 felt I deserved to be punished for being me. Thankfully, she was replaced in the last quarter of the year by a very polite and jolly lady who kept her opinions to herself.

'Pull your socks up, Donna,' said Ms Jones, our Year 4 teacher. Donna bent down and pulled her socks up.

'I didn't mean that. It's an expression,' the teacher told Donna. This was very odd; what did she mean by 'expression'? Looking it up, I understood that adults could say things that had an alternate meaning to what the individual words suggested. These 'games' that adults played seemed to be a waste of energy, but I was keen to find out why they did this and to pretend to do the same amongst them.

'Where does all the smoke from people's cigarettes go? Wouldn't the whole sky be filled with smoke by now, or for that matter, farts?' It took me a few months to arrive at the conclusion that the smoke, just like farts, somehow broke down into smaller components until it became of the same matter as the air around me.

Homework was the hour of stupidity: five minutes of work, followed by fifty-five minutes of explaining to Dad why the homework took only five minutes.

It was 1990 when the world finally caught up with fractions when I asked the substitute teacher for that week, 'If you have one and take away two, doesn't that make the answer 'minus' one?' She told me I wouldn't need that until I reached high school. Later, Jonathon asked me what 'minus one' meant.

'It probably means I owe you one.' I replied to him after thinking about it for a few seconds.

I loved to share what I knew. They thought it was about ego. It never was.

Genius and bullies

More life experiences would fill my young mind, like a constant flow of unwanted guests into what was once a peaceful sun-filled room. These memories consisted predominantly of battles as I wouldn't stop wanting to be accepted by other human beings. The videos would become very loud as the room would be packed with more and more people, so noisy I couldn't think of what I was supposed to be doing with much clarity.

As I got older, controlling the negative ones became a problem. No security was strong enough to get these unwanted guests out of my congested head, and I would be embarrassed to be near others in the fear that they may see what I was seeing.

Being taller than most did not protect me from my classmates and I must commend the bravery of these bullies for aiming so high. Going for the attention was a temptation I could not resist, however bad for me I knew it would be. Eventually, the headmistress called my mother to the school to talk about why I was getting bullied. Sharing any daily occurrences with my mum seemed an idea so foreign that I was shocked that the teachers would call my mother to the school. I had to whimper to Mum that I didn't think I could handle school anymore. A much younger mother replied, 'Only people who are retarded can't handle things. Are you telling me you are retarded?' Maybe I was. 'No,' I responded, as I gathered all the strength I could muster and picked up my bag and got out of the car. 'Have a good day, my son,' she would say kindly. 'You will be fine.'

> **Putting her reply in context,** little Mum was an 8-year-old migrant who spoke only French and Maronite Arabic. She was warmly welcomed outside the school gates after her first day in a foreign country by some young female students, but when they sent her home bleeding and crying,

my grandfather advised her to not bother coming home if she was ever bashed again. The next day, she was ready for the end of day greeting, and with every ounce of her little self, she took them down one by one. Only one sibling went home crying that day, and it wasn't her mentally disabled youngest sister with savant tendencies, but her autistic baby brother after being punched by a schoolgirl.

Grandma—who was part of the first generation of Maronites to live free of the Ottomans after 500 years of oppression—took none of that; finding the girl walking home and slapping her. If you think the story ends there, I must tell you that the girl's mum came over to Grandma's house full of anger, with Grandma slapping her silly as well.

Mum soon took over, looking after her younger brothers and sisters when both her parents were shift working, including her mentally challenged savant sister who has forever remained a 12-year-old, counting leaves in the thousands while singing to memorised ABBA lyrics on any given day.

Desiring to break through the female oppression of her inherited culture, she received support from only her father who clearly favoured her amongst all his children to this day: 'People can take away your wealth and your loved ones,' he would say to Mum, 'but they can never take away what you have acquired up here,' touching his index finger to his temple.

Today I watch him battle with dementia.

Church on Sundays was irritatingly slower than the whole week combined.

The parish priest was Father Sam Simon, a tall man who drew much attention from female parishioners. He was one of the 'great Aussie breed' that I had grown up with and loved throughout my younger years at Greenacre. He would spend an hour outside the church chatting with an endless line of fans. He had so much charisma that it felt as though he singled me out for attention, asking me how I was. An odd question, I did not really answer him until years later when it was explained to me that this question required a response.

Other kids my age would run around, with adults conversing nonsensically to each other yet not moving around like people my age. They must have spent that energy when they were still young, if they ever were. So happy I was for the other kids, but so sad that I knew it would never be me they would ask to stupidly run around with them. Being sad for himself was a feeling of comfort for this child, which would not metastasise into suicidal depression for a few years to come.

'Follow me'

By five, I had been playing the piano for three years and was assigned the title of 'talented', the only gift I knew I had.

One of my first real friends before 'Jason' was entitled 'The Talking Wiz Kid'—with each floppy disk with him representing one game. Most were a joke, but Game 50 involved a series of between ten and fifteen notes, each corresponding with a different letter on the 'wizkid' keyboard; it played a note and you had to play the note back. Each new note would need to be played along with the previous ones which by then had to be memorised. If you got the sequence wrong the 'talking wiz kid' would say with frustration 'please try again', and you were not allowed to progress with the sequence and would have to play the whole sequence again correctly first.

Like some sort of prehistoric car navigation software, he would say with pride and joy to 'follow me' when the notes were played the way in which he had requested.

For many children of clients that came to see Mum for tax advice, finding 'wally' in 'where's wally' would be bizarrely difficult, but this game for them would be almost impossible after a sequence of a few notes. Micah and I simply assumed that the nice kids brought over by Mum's clients were just stupid. Not even little brother could fair too well at this musical game but he loved to sit there while he continuously heard the guy say 'follow me' as I followed him.

Within a few days of spending time with the wiz kid, all Micah was hearing was 'follow me' followed by a 'yes!' from me. It became very tense as the string of notes exceeded known records, and we both were wondering if this sequence would end, and for how long I could keep this up.

One evening, through the yelling of my dad to 'cam tu dinnerrr' and 'turrn zat off', the wiz kid stopped saying 'follow me'. He'd run out of notes to play.

Micah and I looked at each other . . . and then started cheering.

When we finally stopped cheering, quiet Micah looked at me and said two words with the upmost respect:

'Follow me'

'Go to bed boys!' yelled my father from the kitchen.

Even today when I time travel to the past, drag out a memory and recreate it for Micah in the present day, he'll look at me and say, 'Follow me.'

Faith and music

Our older cousins shared our dad as their maternal uncle, and had a mother as stocky as he. They looked unbelievably Middle Eastern but contradicted that look with the most laid back Aussie accents you will ever find outside of Australia's remote habitats. Staunch South Sydney Rabbitoh supporters, they were the children of a polite man of the eastern orthodox faith; a man mistreated by pro-Western successfully capitalistic 1930s Catholic Lebanese Society as a communist. These cousins of mine, closer to me than any human bar my brother were the first to laugh at me for blessing bread I picked up off the floor when being baby sat by them.

It was the first time I ever questioned my faith. I was 7, and it was time to tackle the largest book outside of Mum's 'Hite Report' on female sexuality: the bible.

Warmth filled our home the day my parents brought with them my electronic keyboard. The adults they knew would be fascinated with me playing anything they could whistle to me, whether hearing it before or not. Dad, still built like a freight train and looking like Clark Kent with his 80s glasses would whistle old hymns from the Syriac–Aramaic era of the Maronite church and I would play them, while he sat next to me at the keyboard. These were great times, and I am sure he was impressed with his boy as he would say, 'Zhemy, you arre verry smarret. We know zis when you arre boy.'

It wasn't long before reputation of talent spilled over to Father Sam's doorstep, telling Mum of a teacher just across the road. The lessons were expensive for Mum and Dad, who had only been earning enough to satisfactorily feed their children without themselves going slightly hungry for less than three years.

Harold was very welcoming and wore a type of smile I hadn't seen before, like it was going to burst into a giggle at any moment. He was old to little me, but most likely in his mid to late twenties with a thin frame, black hair, and thick glasses. Due to his dad's vision problems, I had to walk through a dark kitchen and past a yellow-coloured light glowing upon his parents seated in plastic chairs. Harold's studio burst with light and books of music, and his piano was an upright black beauty.

He did well to put up with such an unfocused child, who sat still as little as Harold's parents moved around. Sheet music would jump around on the page before me like rows of karate kicks. All this child could do was hear the music, capture it, then blast it back out onto the piano, thereby bypassing the desire to ever read music.

I stored the sounds in my head and practised them at home as Mum and Dad would close the door to the room where I practised. As the classical pieces became more complex, Harold captured them on tape for me to listen to, learn from, and play back at home. The mountains, Father Sam, and anything else of importance were all fading away very quickly as the creeping in of waves of music cleaned out my mind of all else. I did not want to see the keys as I would turn out the lights and sit before my newly gifted piano to a new world: a brown beauty that I'm sure cost a young Mum and Dad any savings they may have had. As soon as I closed my eyes and touched the keys, the sounds would pull me into the beautiful world outside space and time, where I was in control of the brilliant stream of colours I could see by the sounds I was creating on the engine which kept me in this world. This world was real, logical, controllable, peaceful, and serene. Out there, away from the dream of the human world, I was who I really was—great, important, valuable, and powerful. There was no sadness that was not beautiful, no anger that was harmful nor unacceptable, but angels of colour that would streak past me as I followed them through sound.

Music was so mathematical, logical, pattern focused. Music was all.

'Zhemy put it down, I am on ze phone!'

Interruptions weren't too bad. I knew I would return soon.

I liked Harold, eventually naming him 'Jamie' while he would reply with *'Eimaj'* back. With such an ability to play the piano according to Harold, it was time to head to the conservatory of music to be tested with some classical pieces.

Harold got me the tapes.

SPEED
(My friends, the traffic lights)

The outdoors was freedom, but sports involving other people were not, leaving me with a black BMX that I would ride for hours. At first it was the drive way, then the footpath outside the house, graduating to the end of the street, then around the block not long after. Greenacre was excitingly bigger than the few houses I'd called my neighbourhood, and it allowed me to befriend one other rush—speed.

With speed, the air was fresher, the sun was brighter, and people were nicer. Life would be travelling closer to the speed of my mind, and the wind would caress my face and cool my neck against the sun's rays.

The magical little world of the beautiful Aussies and Maronite elders was now part of something bigger. A world that was much more lifeless, apart from the sounds of the cars starting and stopping at traffic lights. The child and his growingly muscular legs would just watch them change colour, loving to count the many cars that would be stuck at the red light at the local intersection as there were two distinct patterns, the build-up of cars on the quieter road varying much more at different times of the day. Lights made complete sense, and people obeyed them—showing this boy that people must have possessed little or no logic themselves. I wished I could take them with me and when people annoyed me I could just ask them to turn red and say to the people, 'Sorry, you can't cross right now, you are annoying. Come back when the lights turn green.'

Then I'd keep them red for fun.

Despite being surprisingly uncoordinated, there was the exception of handball. I must thank the fence for playing with me for so many years between reading books and riding that BMX.

From 1987 to 1989, Ben Stevens reigned supreme as the school bully; a nice guy at times, he would unusually pick on people other than myself. I hated that he would make the very same people that bullied me feel the way they had when bullying me, and had to stop this. On Mum's advice to stand up against bullies, I approached him when I saw him pushing some younger kid around. Despite not knowing what to do, and shaking terribly, I went up to him and punched him in the chest. Fortunately, I had taken him by surprise and he backed off, as I don't know if I could've done that again.

Weeks later, Ben, still the only kid bigger than me, asked me what type of 'what' was said against his girlfriend by John, a long-time bully of mine from whom I would eventually require adult protection. Two types of 'what' made absolutely no sense, as logic should have dictated a separate word created for the second 'what' by now. My incoherent reply helped Ben take down John regardless, which John swore he would get revenge against me for in the years to come. He stayed true to his word, and I stayed true to being the idiot dragged into being the enemy of those I had no idea were mine.

The Death of Greenacre

Greenacre was still undergoing its transformation from farm land into inner city suburb, where the remnants of Australian farmers existed in the form of the older Anglo-Australians protecting me from abuse from school. They would be the last of the 'Father Sam' generation in this area of Sydney, and no weekend sound was a more attractive siren than the whirring of the old two-stroke lawnmower of a neighbour on a beautiful spring day—followed by the familiar yells from 'Dudley', 'Wally', or 'Frank' inviting Dad over for a beer.

My parents' success was yet unrealised in those days thanks to my dad's great job as a chef and Mum's even better one as a student, and the cosy fibro shack they bought led to the quiet backyard surrounded by fallen, wooden fencing like dead soldiers in 'no man's land'. Through no man's land, I could see only caged pigeons at Khalid's place, and quiet backyards with no people. The fencing and house had more makeovers over time than a rich old actor, eventually materialising an office for Mum and her new business.

If one of the women of Khalid's household ever ventured into their back yard without the hijab on and saw my father through our elevated kitchen window washing dishes, she would run back inside. My dad would be amused by this, and I found it amusing that he found it amusing. Dad would send Khalid his home cooking as I grew up, until the day Khalid uttered the words 'Thank you very much, because anything we can take from you Christians is a blessing from God'.

Dad still invited Khalid and his brother over from time to time.

I was never truly aware of the sectarian divide that ran through the eastern Mediterranean, and that was slowly emerging in western Sydney. My dad did his best to hide the violent sectarian issues he experienced in 1970s Australia between the Mediterranean and Arabic Lebanese, and becoming a house husband helped him hide his past from me until being driven home by him from North East Boys' when I noticed the young mobs attending the newly built Arabic school that would give our cross-bearing vehicle the finger as we travelled past. Lying awake at night, as you now know about, brought with it not only the reconstructing of conversations of days past with better endings but the observing of the light swinging from the ceiling when there was no sign of even a breeze. Perhaps it was due to the earth's rotation or magnetic field.

My father was a lot of fun when Micah and I were little; he would get down on all-fours and we'd ride around on his concrete back. As my protectors died off and as Greenacre descended into an unassimilated mix of cultures and violence, Dad became less patient and started to obsess about most of what we were doing. 'Don't touch that!' or 'be careful!', were common phrases. On one occasion, under severe pressure from himself to impress his in laws, he attempted corporal punishment on us in advance, just in case. He had a temper at times that was equally as impressive as his jovial side that people adored. In his native dialect there would be no accent, and his swearing had a brilliant and destructive power that I both adored and despised—as it seemed to be directed at me more times than I would ever have liked.

Sabrina

I was 8 and she was 12 when I saw her standing at the entrance to Grandma's place with a cute purple dress that went so well with her short and super curly, jet black hair. The sun was blazing through the back entrance, often used as the front entrance, which made her dark olive skin appear even darker. Her massive almond, black eyes were so hard to resist looking at. I felt myself blush and I didn't know what I was feeling, other than that I wanted to sit near her and simply look at her.

Sabrina thought I was an annoying know-it-all who couldn't keep still for more than an instant.

Sabrina's father was a local smash repairer whom Mum's driving would bring us to over the years, letting me never forget that beautiful woman.

It was time to bust out of Greenacre, but not before I'd been granted a scholarship to study and sing with the St Mary's Cathedral Choir. Mum and I compiled a list of pros and cons about going to St Mary's Vs North East Boys'.

I guess this universe will never know what St Mary's would have been like; however, if we had known what was to come during the child's life at North East, I may have chosen differently.

From dream to nightmare

In the process of shaping myself to be understood by the outside world, I had to learn how the outside world thought. I learned how to play a role to make me accepted in that world. By practising doing things in different ways and watching people's reactions, I discovered how I appeared to other people; every action had a reaction. Everything about how I acted was important—how I dressed, walked, spoke—right down to the timing of my speech.

I feared the crowds on the bus that my older self would one day drive future school kids from Greenacre to North East Boys'. The driver would bring us to a larger, darker, deafening quietness that, when combined with the massive trees and falling leaves, made the whole suburb look like the entrance to a haunted mansion.

We filled the primary school playground like large blue, school-capped penguins, with what seemed like hundreds of students thankfully not noticing me sweat profusely. A threatening speech to do with stepping out of line kept me frozen before we were split into different groups as though a concentration camp.

The former bully, John, along with my great friend Jonathan, whose father had recently passed away of a heart attack, briefly sat next to me until we were each dispersed to a different house. This separation felt deliberate.

Jonathan and I would walk to the station together after school, where he would talk to me about his day and I would rant on about concepts he really needed to know. It was three weeks before he became too active in many school activities with his increasing popularity amongst the teachers and students. We resorted to a Friday walk around the ageing Greenacre where I would discuss my newly discovered loneliness at this school of hell, along with which streets in Greenacre were blocked off to traffic and in which direction. Two Fridays passed, and I knew that I would ruin his image by pursuing his friendship when he stopped making contact.

Despite what John had done all those years, I had to defend him against allegations of 'football head John'; even though his head did seem oddly shaped. Even if I could have somehow been able to have let this continue in the form of poetic justice, there was no way I could lose the last part of Greenacre available, no matter how heinous. This line of thinking would in no way prepare me for John now participating in the growing chorus of insults against me. It took many months to piece together the logic behind such a decision, eliminating option after option until arriving at what you may have arrived at intuitively and very quickly. Resentment grew. Why would he accept defence by a former victim of his against others, only to then pretend to dislike that defender when those very same students within only days began turning against me? I decided to insult him. It was the first time I had ever insulted anyone, and hating my own self for it was made infinitely worse by the desire for justice that contradicted my innate lack of ability to enforce it.

'Your dad's gay; all Lebanese dads are gay' was a comment one day uttered by a kid with a Lebanese dad. 'How can he be gay, he's married and has kids,' I responded.

'That's just a cover,' he said. I pictured my dad covering a pet named 'Gay' with a blanket, and then wondered what this kid with such a viewpoint got up to with his dad.

Strange.

Undiagnosed Tourette's proved an itch I could no longer keep private with the arrival of my retired military grandfather from the motherland; blood would flow like a mini creek as he would cut his toenails with garden shears, yet he was terribly upset by the young boy's strange behaviour. I promised not to repeat it and would hold on with dear life until the next explosion of syllables would bring him down, and bring me down to a new level of self-hatred.

The first time I called out spontaneously in class was the second day at North East and it was in Mr McLean's class. I liked Mr McLean; he wore light-coloured shirts with short sleeves showing off a significant amount of dark hair on his forearms while wearing his flared pants purchased directly from the 1970s. He would try to be angry, although not very good at it, as my first ever syllable explosion filled his room with both disruption and laughter. The decade-long secret was out, and it quickly became an impulse I could not control.

The class cheered when Mr McLean finally gathered the courage to lay down a detention for the Tourette's. An instant rush of excitement bubbled beneath my skin shortly before anger arrived, followed by the embarrassment; a place where I was most comfortable having deserved the outcome for unwillingly interrupting education with an impulse unable to be controlled.

Despite losing almost all self-worth by age 10, drops of encouragement could be found at times: 'What did you say, Jamie? . . . I really would like you to repeat that word you just used to the class.' The word was nefarious. It was not a complex word to the 10-year-old who still assumed it a common word amongst his peers. 'It's very interesting that you use that word. . .'

He asked me where I'd learned it.

'I heard it on Teenage Ninja Turtles and then looked it up in our World Book dictionary.'

If he ever used the word 'bad' from then on, he would look at me and say 'nefarious' and smile.

A final warning for the year was not to alienate others in Year 5 as we may end up without friends in Year 12.

I had plenty of time.

EDDIE
(The bashing of a 10 year old)

It was a perfectly sunny Saturday in a rougher part of Greenacre where we had been playing soccer for two years now, with younger me now finally able to kick a ball and in the right direction as well. My favourite cousin and Mum's nephew and godson, Isaiah, and I had just won our match against great odds and had decided to kick some goals after the crowds had left. The day was as though the last days of term at school when many people didn't bother showing up, allowing peace to take their places.

A massive 16-year-old named 'Eddie' greeted us with a smile and a massive belly, wanting to play against us, and yet and despite his size being greater than the both of us combined, we each scored a goal against him when he scored none back. The only goal I had ever scored in my life brought on a feeling of ecstasy that may have not been so intense but for the sadness that had engulfed me for such a long time. Unable to regulate the intensity of the joy he felt, young Jamiel did nothing but cheer when Eddie asked him to come over. Isaiah yelled in unison with me as I happily jogged over to big Eddie. I remember him there in his white T shirt and red shorts, then finally realising that Isaiah wasn't yelling with me but was instead warning me to get away......

'Don't go over there. . .!'

It was too late.

I had a split second to wonder why Eddie stated that I slept with mothers, before feeling an astounding electric shock, followed by my head moving involuntarily away from my left shoulder; ripping my neck muscles apart to the tune of a distant scream to get away by a very disturbed Isaiah. Before I could process what was occurring, I felt another electric shock and more neck muscles tear, only this time to the opposite side. The last I remember was being confused at what was going on whilst seeing the green grass move towards me, followed by pitch black.

When I came to, the sunny and peaceful day had returned. I couldn't hear anything.

Tears were mixed with dirt on my face, while my hearing slowly returned along with Isaiah's yelling. Not understanding what we had done to deserve such violence, I got up. I could walk. Sifting through indeterminate yelling, the 10-year-old stumbled towards the tuck shop shelter where a younger and smaller team mate with the face and haircut of a 'norrty boy', as Dad would call it, was leaning against the brick wall with his arms folded and one leg behind his back. This popular-looking kid asked me why I hadn't thumped him back. I told him I thought it was best to turn the other cheek, which had him buckle over with laughter, probably because I was hit on both sides of my face.

I didn't know what the normal kids would have done differently, but I knew at that point a rage, and fear, I had never known.

Based on Eddie's age, the 10-year-old calculated that he had five years before the other kids would start applying equivalent or even greater physical harm and still without knowing why he was causing so much hatred and animosity towards himself.

I had to protect myself to the point where I could defeat Eddie.

In fact, I decided I would again face this monster and show him the same courtesy he showed me that day. Most likely being swayed by the usual and repeated hostility of the North East Boys as I travelled between lunch and the classroom, I got hold of a martial arts book; practising in the safety of my room each day until my fists and legs would bleed. Weekends would now see me ride my new mountain bike to Nathaniel's house and train on his boxing bag until the sun went down. Over the months my body became stronger, and more flexible. The seed of hatred had been planted, and the soil was not that bad.

Harold was adamant on the conservatory. His unusual level of excitement had given me the energy to repeat the classical pieces he had left for me on cassette tapes two years prior, until what I heard myself playing on my piano was identical to the versions I was listening to. On the day of the exam, my parents and Micah waited outside for the forty-five minutes to tick away. The examiner, an old man in his late thirties, asked me why I hadn't opened the sheet music. He assured me it was okay that I had memorised the pieces that I began to perform, one by one. The parents of the girl being tested simultaneously were proudly chatting to my parents when I reappeared amongst them.

She had received an A which was very impressive.

I had received an A+, and thereby a perfect score by memory.

My parents were joyous beyond anything I had expected and may have forgotten to continue speaking with the parents of the girl thereafter. The increase in bullying to follow this day would coincide with the withdrawal from the study of music by 13.

Remember Mr Stuart with the mullet from the 1980s TV beer ad? 'What do you love Jamiel? Tell the headmaster what you love.'

I sat there saying nothing until the class joined in and I decided to accept the attention being offered to me: 'Behind the news' which always got a laugh from the rest of the class.

'The less BTN you give most kids is a reward; with Jamiel, if you want to punish him you take it away,' sang Mr Stuart, with the class following him in chorus.

When he told me to 'hurry up or I'll take away your BTN homework', I hurried up. They had no idea of the value of the knowledge stemming from that great show, but the attention was sickeningly addictive.

I know that my social skills were once more inadequate than most; today I like to think they are far more heightened than most, simply because I had to learn them.

Everyone changes—cell by cell, and over the years we transform. What makes us what we are gradually disappears and is replaced. It's like a crowd of people—take one person out of the crowd and replace them with another the perceived crowd is still there.

Computers, suicide, and people

The 12-year-old's few obsessions would have continued but for Mum making the mistake of leaving her new office PC unattended. This was before Windows was a common interface, leaving me to interact with the text-based 'DOS'. I would type the command, and it would comply. The fact that this made complete sense, made no sense at all.

My commands were exactly understood, and this PC was completely intuitive to use. Nothing was intuitive to use? I had to keep exploring this PC until I could find out why we knew each other so well. This lasted for a very quick hour, followed by me unintentionally destroying its configuration system. Mum's computer guy let me watch him rebuild it, leaving me with the ability to modify, amend, and recreate the entire configuration system. Whilst not replacing the desire for the human company I hated for showing me how to hate myself, I had found a new friend. The next step was to take my new friend apart when Mum was at meetings; rebuilding it many times over with one part missing each time. Rebuilding and upgrading PCs became a great pastime for both me and my brother.

Forcing us to spend time with other people saw Mum and Dad enrol us into a holiday programme. Old friend David was there, along with a now almost 180-cm-tall Jamiel for whom the children provided unending reverence. Games had to be changed often as the kids would follow my tactics to win games that proved too discreet for even David and Micah to think to implement. Reverence proved to be an anticlimax, but that overload of social experience suggested that it was easier to get along with people either much older or much younger.

Pretending to be normal was difficult at best but did minimise the bullying; and although I would promise myself I would maintain it indefinitely, I knew this was not yet in my control. Like a smooth road with the odd bumps, there would appear laughing at the wrong moment, a word said too loud, or no laugh when one was required. One common pattern noticed was when one kid would tell a story before other students with an outcome that could have been understood in more than one way. Caught off guard, I would explain this to them, only to be made shockingly aware that these multiple answers were both implied and inferred.

With the social dysfunction becoming increasingly apparent, I would fall into depression whilst pondering on how to do a better job with the next opportunity. I had to get there. I gave myself until 17.

Jason passed on during the first year of high school. I wasn't comfortable taking money from Mum to replace his batteries, if I had known where to find some, and my spare change included only left over pieces after buying the milk and newspaper for Dad.

Sitting in the toilets during the lunch hour proved a peaceful habit before building up the courage to enter the library to spend time with 'authors'. The nonfiction quenched my thirst for knowledge, whilst the fiction taught me about how kids seemed to interact with one another. At age 12, I turned to the absolutely fascinating world of physics.

Of all the things the contemptable Mr Stuart could have predicted correctly, it had to be acne.

I made a fifteen-minute, B-grade martial arts video with Isaiah for a competition advertised to us by our art teacher. He was a caring girl, and one of the rare adults around us more interested in those who were less interested in conformity. The bloopers made the story, but the tall, lanky, acne-congested face bound by a metal jaw strap asked me *'why have any self-respect anymore?'* which felt good, like a professional athlete who no longer can compete and so can finally eat that burger. Go on . . . it tastes *good*.

FOUR EYES

There was something wrong with the stove clock. It seemed blurry. It turned out that I needed glasses, and I chose some really cool glasses with rims the size of a car's wheels. Constantly putting and taking the glasses on and off, repeatedly, trying to memorise the differences between both pictures was how I would not take for granted the blanket of blur that had developed with deteriorating sight. The blurry hue was a spherical cocoon; protecting against the chaotic world just on the other side.

The blur would put more focus on recognising others by the way they walked before putting on the glasses for the result. Not only did every person's walk carry a different signature, but guys from unrelated social groups would share similar strides. They didn't notice this in the same way my younger self had no idea of his starkly deviated walking pattern. Ultimately, it was less of a burden not to recognise others and thereby avoid the practice of repeating the word hello to the same people throughout the day, a concept as ridiculous as the idea of saying 'purple bricks' as many times.

"Purple Bricks, again, friend!"
"Purple bricks, buddy"
How Ridiculous.

A growing boy needed bigger glasses, and these new glasses gave the young man the look of an evil nerd. Years later and I still could not believe that Mum looked at those glasses and thought, 'Yes, these will make Jamiel look good.' In all fairness to her, I also thought they were going to get me a girl from the bus ride home until the guys on the bus collapsed onto the floor laughing as soon as immaculately dressed, evil nerd arrived.

Constant ridicules by both students and teachers, the beatings, the stickers on my back, the throwing down the stairs by Muhammed in 1986 which teenage me had actually forgotten about for a while, the disgusting notes written to teachers by other groups of kids on my behalf, having to spend lunch in the toilets waiting for the day to pass. My first suicide note that a teacher caught was in Year 7. Young Mr Simons did read it, but never spoke to me about it and thankfully did not tell anyone until parent-teacher night many months later. Mum was unbelievably appalled but said nothing to me with the only change noticed being the unrelated resignation from the school by Mr Simons. I needed to kill myself but had gotten away with surviving this time.

Bullies get bigger
So I guess you have no choice

Peter Barry was a huge rugby-playing bully who brought into my life an evolved anxiety. He liked to puff out his chest and sometimes rub his man breasts in an almost ape-like fashion. Without surprise, the teachers loved him and I, in turn, despised them further. I hated how he made me scared to get out of the car in the mornings, and how I couldn't sleep, not wanting the day to end with the next morning's rise and the pummelling by Peter that would follow suit. Saturday evening was where the fears would beg me to pump a knife through my chest, as the next day would be Sunday which meant that Monday was coming: day 1 out of 5 of threats, filthy and racist remarks, and stuff given to me by Mum and Dad being stolen from me. According to P. Barry, my pants were worn at a height that he was surprised wasn't strangling me (which in hindsight he was right about) and he would make sure that no one spoke to me for fear of reprisal by him. I was a disease.

School was the hell of hells, and the motherless home with the controlling Dad watching our every single move like an eagle cross-bred with Superman was like escaping from a gas chamber and into a furnace. Sneaking up to my room and practicing beating a Peter/Eddie hybrid to death until he was one punch away from a fractured hand, this child in a young man's body hated himself so much for wanting to hurt those who hurt him, and despite his limited facial expressions, he desired nothing but to scream until his voice box burst out of him and into a hole which would swallow both it and him into oblivion. He even started stepping on cracks in the hope that they would do to him what he feared they would do to him as a child.

When Dad found out, his answer was talk to Peter's father and we'd all be friends. I was horrified at the ridiculous suggestion. Let me quickly put that into context:

> **1986** saw a 5-year-old being sent to Arabic class for the first time, and when Dad asked how my first day was I explained that an older boy named Muhammed was a new friend, but a little strange as he threw me around the room after class. The next morning was when Dad spoke to young Muhammed:
>
> 'You arrre a good boys,' he pleaded with the smiling Muhammed and his entourage, 'Please look aftarrr my son. He iz good boy and good friend tu yu.'
>
> 'Don't worry,' replied Muhammed with a lovely smirk, 'we will take good care of him'.
>
> That was the day Muhammed grabbed me by the neck, shook me violently, and then threw me down the concrete stairs.
>
> You may see why 13-year-old Jamiel would have been horrified by Dad's suggestion.

Twelve months of bullying by P. Barry were coming to a close, and I put suicide on hold whilst huddled on a corner couch at my grandparents' new place up the coast, reading *Evolution versus Creationism*. Mum's extended family decided to loudly brainstorm the bullying situation. I thoroughly enjoyed that book.

Never witnessing adults brainstorming prior to this unusual day, and to witness adults worse at it than a headless chicken gave me even less hope about avoiding a confrontation with Barry. The humorous dialogue as well as evolutionary theory vs Genesis was a combined topic I was ranting on about some weeks later when being minded once again by Dad's strong shouldered sister. Her youngest son, John, had just completed high school and I'd always seen him as a popular guy given any situation with guys or girls. As standard procedure, he would sift through my rants without me realising and reply:

'Jamiel . . . I know what everyone's telling you,' he said calmly whilst I stopped chatting and continued reading on his mum and Dad's couch; 'When I was at school, there were a few guys who gave me a pretty hard time.' This was certainly hard to believe, but I still waited for the predictable chorus of forgiveness or the 'parent-to-parent reconciliation' speech.

'To this day,' he went on, 'I wish I could go back, line them all up with a baseball bat . . . and belt the living s*** out of them—one by one. . .'

Dad's sister and her strong shoulders bolted into the room as though she had been hawking us the whole time.

'John do not say zis to Jamie!' screamed Aunty Jennifer who even John assumed had just materialised out of nowhere. 'Jamie is good boy, do not make bad soughts in his mind!'

'Mum, he's gotta hear it from someone,' replied John quite calmly, 'or else he's just gonna keep getting abused.'

I let them fight amongst themselves while I started to contemplate what John had said.

Adolescent Jamiel, who attracted abuse for even the way he walked, decided he had three options at that point:

Option 1. Living with the abuse
Option 2. Suicide

Or

Option 3. Killing his soul through violence against another human being.

He decided to hold onto suicide as the last resort.

The depression was getting worse. School holidays saw me immobilised for days in my room, permitting the videos to annex reality whilst trying to analyse why people acted the way they did towards me.

Self-deprecation devolved into playing my Boys to Men CD over and over again in pitch blackness. It kept me alive for the next few years.

With Sabrina tucked away at that point, I first saw the love of my life on the third last day of school's bus ride home for that year, not long before I would be on a plane with Mum, Dad, and Micah on the way back to the Mediterranean. A dark-eyed, thick brown-haired, olive-skinned dancer that made my heart almost stop; she sat before me where all I could do was remember to breathe. With her own gravitational pull, no one else seemed to be affected by her almond-shaped eyes.

My stop was here, but she remained on the bus so I guess my stop had not yet arrived.

This was not good. Home at a later time would throw out the routine which would amplify the depression. This torturous thought lasted for three stops, with the massive pounding in my chest almost closing my airways. *Am I stalking someone now, or am I just her "protector"?* I thought to myself in between noticing my shaking hands and sweaty palms. *No, she won't notice just like Mum didn't notice Dad,* whilst walking five metres behind her.

She stopped walking for a moment, looked slightly upwards, as if to cock her ears in a certain direction, and then spun around.

At this point, I was compelled to bend down and tie my already tied left shoelace.

Dropping further behind her, she disappeared 'round the corner. Despite running not to lose sight of her, no ground between us was gained; strange. Not wanting to seem obvious, I ran back the way I came and went home.

This would, of course, make the next day at school the longest of my life. No memories of bullying can be remembered for that day and what felt like a month later, the most beautiful woman in existence was before me once again on that bus. Now I couldn't wait to get off the bus with the most amazing person in the world. Rehearsing the same line all day was now ready to be uttered without throwing up:

'*I* . . . *m* . . . *really sorry* . . . *to bug you, but I* . . . *just had* . . . *to ask you your name.*' The edges of her pursed lips began to elevate above the centre of them at the same time as the edges of her exotic eyes started doing the same. I think that meant a smile. She smiled!

'My name is Jessica'.

'*My name is Jamiel, Jessica,*' I responded with what was hopefully a smile, but complete control of facial expressions had not yet been mastered by then.

'Nice to meet you, Jamiel,' she replied with pure grace. I immediately ran back home, not feeling a thing except the warm glow in my chest that had only ever ignited during my child's version of myself in the far away mountains. Ladies and gentlemen, we have found a cure . . . and her name is Jessica.

A few days later, Mum and Dad took us to a white Christmas in the ancestral mountains where Australia and that life I had lived since leaving was a faint idea at best.

I loved noticing the time of sunset in the mountains and how it differed to the time of sunset on the coast. The amount of love I had for meeting new family members was as much as my mother's desire to never return. Taken everywhere under the pretext of an older cousin's hot 18-year-old boyfriend taught me that 'hot' meant 'good', but I wasn't 18?

Mum's decade-long financial struggle with Dad by her side saw a defeat for the struggle, and a leap into a new home.

Now with our own rooms, Micah and I could both see and hear the Adidas-wearing teenagers and their loud cars.

Guys spoke about female body parts on the bus ride home, and you better believe that I was going to emulate them without them even noticing. My 'hot' older female neighbour whose existence I was not yet sure of was the topic I would lead them with, and *'Yeah she's got all those things'* was my response to Mark while I struggled to keep my upper body further away from these boys than my waist as they seemed to do. I was in with the guys. It was a sure thing.

The above video tells a much older Jamiel a very different story.

Mark seemed unusually excited to hear this unorthodox acting kid with jerky movements talking about the fairer sex he had in no way come near since being born out of one, which was actually due to both he and his mate fully aware of a good-looking 16-year-old school girl sitting right behind this kid.

The first feeling that I may have made a mistake arrived upon noticing an older girl following me off the bus. The feeling matured as she was still behind me when walking into my new street. When she followed me into the driveway, I just knew I had to say something.

'Were you sitting behind me on the bus?' I asked with a matter of fact.

'Yes,' she replied with a smile.

Being a loser in front of the younger Mark, and now in front of the opposite sex, had a comfortingly degenerative effect on the remaining shreds of my desire to live.

There was no way this semi-coordinated boy who looked forward to each sporadic moment of social success would be able to speak to Jessica ever again, but his need to be in touch with her helped him entrust Mark from the bus to hand her his hand-written letter letting Jessica know 'how beautiful you are'.

There had to be a way to talk to her, I thought, as I was walking from the school to the station. At that point I saw a sign.

The sign was hanging from Jessica's College wall for a dance they were holding.

I could barely hear Dad warning me 'not to liv u drrrink wayrr iz ozerr peopl' as I disappeared into the blinding lights and deafening noise. This was the first time I had been this close to girls, and they held my gaze hostage from the word go: conversations, numerous facial expressions, friendships, and crowds. Why did boys' schools exist?

Sitting at the end of a row of seats with a can of lemon soda that I couldn't drink for fear that it had been spiked was when I saw her.

Jessica's elegant demeanour from the centre of her circle of friends had my hands tingling in all its natural beauty and through her I was sure that friends would now become a reality. The noise was pushing my mind over the edge.

Interrupted by Jessica being dragged towards me by her tiny friend, I tried to keep breathing. The noise, the people everywhere, they were all accepted. What was I doing here with these ordinary human beings? What could I possibly say once Jessica was pushed over here? Why was she being pushed if my love was not unrequited?

It's a dance. It just occurred to me that they would then be expecting me to dance; people were moving in illogical sequences with patterns I could not yet recognise. There was no time for this. How did her friends know my name as they came dreadfully close to my space at the corner of the room with the spiked drink in my hand about to fall to the floor? Something had to be done.

'Is it true that you followed her home?' yelled her tiny friend who I had just realised was also very good looking, over the bass thumping through the large speakers across the dance floor. I did my best to avoid looking at Jessica while not understanding the question. Were they perhaps implying that Jessica was inaccurate in her understanding of the day we met?

Jessica was dragged closer, and my body had clearly decided what to do without informing me; springing out of the makeshift club like a bunny rabbit avoiding landmines, not knowing what effect this would have on any chance with either Jessica or her tiny friend. Desperation was taking over after heading back in and then bolting out for a second time when asked to dance by the very same group in the same way.

He didn't know what an anxiety attack was at that age, but the disease was enough to render the rest of his night a blank page as he sat away from the beating bass and fully functioning students, hugged by the blackness of night and the outer school wall which made a comfortable corner with the carpark tarmac. It stayed that way till a girl called his name from not too far away. He was so excited that a person was looking for him, until they explained that a lady claiming to be his mum was in her blue sports shirt and black tights looking for me.

In a desperate attempt to save face, he asked her why she would embarrass him by entering the premises.

Very close to my age now, Mum must have struggled to remain strong while her little boy who was now much bigger than her seemed in more need of love than he did as an actual child. The haunting memories of this evening would always be with him. Jessica was gone.

Waiting for the bus back to Greenacre, her friends filed passed me with a 'Hello Jamie!' one by one. Mortified whilst simultaneously devouring the poisonous attention like a starving dog, I crouched down onto my bag and looked at the ground.

My second suicide note asked Jess to be at my funeral which was handed to her by Mark, who had been chatting with Jess for quite a while, now walking her home each day from then on.

I continued to pray for the courage to end this wrecked life of disease that needed to un-exist before tragedies gained momentum on a larger scale. The saved up first kiss was squandered on a girl met on a subsequent family holiday and although younger than me, she seemed to know what she was doing.

The pit and the power

Calculators were brilliant, but banned, despite the codes and patterns that could be created with them. After multiple enforcements of the banning, it was young me that switched off.

With the so-called 'maths' going on in their world, I was absorbed in the amazing book before me, explaining the linguistic and cultural origins of names that inspired me to discover these new cultures at home. Our substitute teacher was filling in during the days that I was most absorbed by this book. He would get on quite well with the popular boys, of course.

Asking me if he could see the book from the other side of the room, I assumed he was testing his eyesight. Happy with the request, I replied, 'Sure, if you can see that far.'

Not knowing why the whole class had erupted with laughter, I once again mimicked them by laughing along.

D level maths must have been the right choice, I guess. This insane, new world was asking me to work for the same marks I was once attaining for free. No longer giving a single shred of damn, I walked into the final exam having been force fed a summary of the maths year by Mum.

Surprisingly I was the only person in the year to score 100 per cent in the final section of the exam, dedicated to 'problem solving'.

Asking me to stand up before the school mates who were always ready to pounce, the teacher with the voice of God asked me if I knew what I had done. Knowing this teacher to have whipped my uncle during his tenure at school during the 1970s, I prayed that I hadn't done anything. Mr 'God Voice' went on to explain what I had mentioned earlier, declaring it as something that could not be taught. Punishing the class with admiration for my supposed extreme abstract thinking, I hoped that this would at least get me one friend. Like opening an airplane door during mid-flight, the bell sucked the students out of the classroom, leaving me with the always loyal depression, and an upgrade to B mathematics.

The growing boy was baptised with names he did not choose for himself, ultimately forgetting his own. Conditioned to despise himself by his desire to be accepted by humanity, his rage was growing.

My questions were now always 'for later', leaving my thirst for more to become only the more ravenous. These questions were not for later, but for now so that there would be time for more questions later. I despised myself for needing love from those whom I so despised, and whose banal conversations were completely foreign to me, but intelligible to each other.

This school needed to be punished, with the tactic now evolving into asking any question I could; knowing full well that no question would ever be answered, forever fuelling me with the energy to pummel the classroom with even more questions. This newly discovered strength within me both scared and excited me with the feeling of power that came with it.

From victim to bully

There were now only martial arts, speed cycling, and reading more about people; filling the void between oases of comments acknowledging my unusual level of physical fitness. Through my mountain bike and a lot of time, I was discovering new and beautiful landscapes, further and further afar.

Dad would say, 'Tell Uncle Rrraymond allo forr me' and I would ride there and tell Uncle Raymond that my dad said hello, and he would ask me to say hello back, leaving me to ride straight back home to tell Dad the good news.

Over and over in each day, I would share my dad's greetings with family members located across the vast flatness of Sydney. After riding the sixteen kilometres round trip to Isaiah's place in fourteen minutes, Micah baptised me—'the machine' as he hung on for dear life to the back of my bike whilst wearing his roller blades.

Taking packets of chips with me on solo adventures, I once stopped to eat one while wearing my tight green fluoro shirt and rainbow-coloured shorts the day that two teenagers, one Islander Australian and one Anglo-Australian, approached me. I was delighted to hear them greet me with a 'Hi' and could not comprehend why they then warned me to get out of their street. I just froze, wondering if they may be screaming at someone behind me and was almost witnessing them from outside my body bring their threats closer as though I was simply the audience.

Like at the dance where I so smoothly bolted out of the room, my legs jumped onto the bike, leaving the plastic chips bag on the floor as the guys started kicking the rear tyre of my bike. After being so distressed at the thought of littering, I begged the gigantic legs beneath me to tell me why they didn't take those boys down as quickly as they pedalled away, whilst only briefly wondering why strangers would want to hurt me. The child could only surmise that these gangsters must have had connections to the school kids and were perhaps asked to hurt him if he was sighted.

After almost three years of martial arts training, it dawned on young Jamiel that it was not enough to know it in theory, and he realised that it was now time to use it.

The anger would pulsate through my vein-covered arms and would only oscillate like a pendulum between my upper and lower body. Dissipate it would never, and the anger only made me more angry. I was disgusted at my desire for vengeance upon Eddie, Peter, the gangsters, the teachers, the kids, and upon myself for letting this happen; wanting only to sit in the woods beyond the great lion heads, watching the sun stream through the trees—with no memories, no anger, and no videos.

Suicide note number 3 arrived in Year 8. *'I want to die'*. My gym teacher wrote back, 'See me after class.'

I saw him after class through the open doorway to his office, laughing with popular kids. Serious was I as serious he was not. I walked off, and he never asked me about it again.

Two years of torture via the talking ape, Peter Barry, had now concluded. Although still taller than me, I was now unsure of what I was capable; with this muscular 13-year-old, six-foot male now performing the splits side on against the wall during the inception of some classes. Kicks were destroying Nathaniel's punching bags, and punches were now focused on palm trees at speeds that made even Nathaniel's father Raymond applause. Any day now would be the day I would finally react.

Jamiel, now an almost 14-year-old man with a baby blonde beard that he let grow during the holidays had a fear of himself that helped him feel safe against others he should have feared more. The first venting of that fear came through a crack in his composure, the day he stared at Peter Barry's chin and said, *'Mate, you'd better watch it; one day I'm going to lose my temper.'* Jamiel was visibly shaking from that very fear; scared of what would happen if he were to be consumed by the rage incubated within him like a venomous reptile ready to hatch.

I didn't want to be angry. I wanted everyone to be friends. My friends.

The day the reptile hatched commenced no differently from any other. Bullying one of his own followers, I spluttered a line from a movie I'd recently seen, asking him with more fear than I'd ever felt to "*...pick on someone his own size*".

I didn't mean myself, but that didn't change his gaze of fire which locked onto me as he headed straight towards me while throwing his massive fist at my face. Like handball, time slowed right down and the past three years of training was before my eyes all at once.

I blocked the punch with my left arm and within seconds we were surrounded by others, watching the smaller guy withstanding the force of Barry's fridge-like arm with seemingly no effort whilst resting his right forearm against an empty bag rack. Frustrated, Barry threw his massive fist at me again, which again I blocked. His reign of bullying was about to come to an end.

The theatrics proved too interesting for the extremely tall Brad, who now entered the battle. 'Cool, block this,' he said and was further impressed when I did. Now too proud of myself to notice Peter's fist before it hit my face, my head finally bounced back from the crowd like a soccer ball kicked by a child. I'd had enough and walked in the direction of the year master's office with the long-awaited proof to have Peter Barry expelled. Nothing prepared me for what the next sentence flung across the hall by a random student would do to my legs.

'Levant, you've got blood on your face.' I could feel the warmth of it on my face, whilst looking at the red ooze covering my hand that had just touched it. The year master was going to have to wait.

Older me can still see Peter's face when the younger me turned around. I have now learned that he wore the face of someone who knew what was coming. In less time than in an instant, I galloped through the sea of people staring in unison right at me. Time froze as any student in that hall became a statue for me to pass by, with Barry's jaw dropping further with each stride by the beast he had created. With my last stride I leaped through the air, and right at the bully whose life was about to change for the better.

Like a massive tree about to fall with the last blow from the huntsman's axe, gravity brought me back towards the ground as my bulging right leg landed squarely into the weak point below Barry's hip, bringing him closer to ground—but I had only started.

Each landing of my leg into this dying beast felt better than the one before, and the outflow of rage showed no signs of ceasing. It was only Jonathan who could stop this descent into a murderous rampage, holding me back whilst the anger escaped violently through my legs which were no longer on the ground; using Jonathon's weight to express a level of skill and violence that the students would never forget throughout my remaining years at the school.

During the lunch hour, a student sat next to me.

'I heard you smashed Peter.'

I continued eating my lunch, waiting for this stranger to ask a question. This statement began to repeat itself via the mouths of others.

Although remaining bitter towards me, Peter Barry no longer bullied me, nor anyone else for that matter and eventually treating me as a colleague during the last year of high school. It was now time to be less fearful of even bigger students in older grades, when a stereotypical Australian with Lebanese parents received insults from me after he had kicked my ball out of the handball court, where—by the way—I could now be without Peter Barry's consent. As this older bully came to kick me in the legs, I jumped into the air and lay both my knees simultaneously into his chest. Impressively, he remained standing for a moment, before barely stumbling back to his designated play space. Looking up at the spectator stand, I saw the arms of my peers raised in the air whilst they were chanting my last name as though we were in ancient Rome.

"LE-VANT…LE-VANT…LE-VANT…LE-VANT…"

The beast within me raised my arms parallel to the tennis court ground as though the remaining Gladiator before his slain enemy.

If I got to class early enough, I could now sit at the back of the room.

A monster was growing within me, and I loved it.

Which Christianity

Melody and Todd were two of our neighbours' three children, knocking on our door with a request for us at their gathering that evening. Without any school uniforms, it took a while to adjust to the scene.

Natalie exuded a fragrance of confidence as she lay almost motionless on the couch. I wasn't ready to sit amongst my peers as of yet, and from the ground, I could learn from the others more discreetly.

Melody and Todd's father was a pastor of Maronite descent, who my older self has since realised had had his children sent over as soldiers to grab 13-year-old Micah and me away from the sin of Catholicism.

The first game they played involved quoting scripture. If not the attention of the voluptuously, brown-skinned Natalie with skin more beautiful than liquid-gold caramel, it was the crowd's—which was had by me quoting biblical verses by memory and on demand.

If anything was learned by 15, it was to share only a few words with Natalie and hope that no strangeness appeared in that time. Not talking enough was a new lesson learned, where an adult self can see that teenage Jamiel had her engaged when he thought he had not and walking away helped in turn to do the same. His trashed self-image was a product of the past but destroyed his present and gave him no hope for the future.

Crawling back to his room after the party was over, the darkness, the CD, and the depression were forever waiting.

Micah was always gifted with the ability to walk away from people, leaving me to ride the twenty kilometres each Sunday to listen to more anti-Catholic rhetoric, justified by the same bible I had now read a few times from cover to cover over the last seven years. Gifted with the power of logic without any intuitive emotional understanding, it was easy to see where their arguments against the Catholic Church and its doctrines were consistent with reality, before they would then dive back into the supernatural for their own, logic-independent solutions to world problems. The final straw came after Mum and her four-wheel drive had been flipped over by a lawless driver. As opposed to collectively and proactively getting involved in somehow helping, they decided to join a pastor-led prayer and do nothing else, while Dad, like a runaway truck, would stop at nothing to get through the wreckage to his wife—unable to be stopped by all the fire fighters combined.

Now being able to see what Micah had seen long before, their group fuelled by its sectarianism and detailed knowledge of a world that was as real to me as the Kingdom of Mount Olympus, I stayed at the fringe of the group with a chubby, blonde teenager called Ben. I would copy his jokes but without hearing laughter after them, whilst we enjoyed talking about ways to kill ourselves. He felt Jesus would forgive him, where I felt he would not for leaving my parents with a messy, disfigured body.

He always commanded not to put the Lord to the test, but that night I took the chance to test Jesus by standing in a black tracksuit in front of an oncoming bus. I closed my eyes as I was increasingly engulfed by the blinding lights of the oncoming bus that made no effort to move off its trajectory. Turning to my side, I looked forward to the ticket out of this nightmare and into the presence of the Jesus inculcated within me since birth.

The rush of the diesel engine was now upon me, and I was ready. Wait.

Was Jesus on the side of the Catholics or these new religious freaks? Damn it. I couldn't take that risk.

The clearest heart startle of the evening was the feeling of the bus's wake like a punch of air from the largest possible concert speaker as I took only one step back from being dead. The deathly quiet awoke me back into reality, and I moved to the grass at the side of the now quiet main road and sat down—watching life move on as usual.

Before receding away from the new Christians, one more step back from the Catholic Church and back to my darkened, music-filled room, I did win a sprint for the Baptist team against others around the state. It was nice to have friends again, and I looked forward to the next opportunity, whenever and however it would appear.

Amen.

Old David

With Jonathan on his way to be a school captain, a new chance for a friend came when David's time at North East was to begin. The guy that stuck with me in primary school was here to save my life. He would prove to them all that I was a good guy. It was the fifth day when he called me at home to say that he could no longer be my friend in public as his new friends didn't like me. Horrified and needing more than anything to be ripped away from this body, it was time to transfer this pain to others. A show once had an audience laugh where a hand shake zapped a man, and I was sure that if I replicated this with thumb tacks attached to my hands when shaking the hands of others, there would be new-found laughter and friends to follow. Unfortunately the pain did not leave, but created only more in others.

The school was a place to move from group to group, mimicking the characteristics of the kids within each one; recording how many days it would take before I was shoved aside. There was much to learn, with a glimmer of hope that I would ultimately prevail, as nights and weekends would see rage pumping through me on the most beautiful of days, leaving me to scream muffled obscenities into pillows.

My grandfather, whom I had only recently discovered and who was a retired anti-Islamic extremist terror operative in the forever diminishing western civilisation of the mother land, was now dying from the effects of smoking since age 12. My own father's cooking was missed when he went back to the mountains to look after his dying dad, surrounded by maturing grapes beneath the alpine sun by day and the numinous milky way by night.

The death of this assassin who shared my name, my blood and had gathered both Muslim and Christian families together at his funeral, brought the monster within me to even faster maturity; pushing boundaries of classroom behaviour much further than I ever would dare do alone. The kids progressed into dreams as their abuse had mutated into a much more malignant form, where nothing was direct but the disease that was young Jamiel for them still existed for them to avoid under pain of death. Pranks were now anonymous, leaving my 15-year-old self not knowing which face was the enemy. A volcanic eruption of rage after weeks of pranks from hidden terrorists had me then walk through the playground, punching anyone I saw. Jamiel remained a child whilst it was the monster that grew into this body that was now attracting the attention of females without his knowledge.

It took only eight months of bullying by the next verminous student for the monster to be released again. He was in the grade below, a lot smaller in stature and with vile comments being spat forth from him whenever we crossed paths. The Eddie-fuelled monster living with me would have most likely waited for two years to pass as it did with Peter Barry, but the bully made the mistake one day of kicking me.

It wasn't me that ran after him, but the 15-year-old recently selected as a state sprinter; the monster that begged to take care of me when I refused. Once the legs beneath me that even final-year students would now comment on during soccer matches ran after him, I knew the rage had taken over. Seeing the bully run from the beast was compelling and I could not look away as his left hand wrapped itself around the bully's neck in an instant, with his right hand now like a jackhammer, destroying the bully's face and chest over and over for each day and each week that he enjoyed tormenting young Jamiel the way that Barry and Eddie had done before him. The monster could see nothing but the memories of him spitting on Jamiel, swearing at Jamiel, vomiting forth inhumane remarks, and laughing at him with his audience of peers.

The bully could no longer stand on his own, but the beast continued to hold him in view of its right hand for further punishment until I tore myself away from my compulsion to keep watching, past his immobilised friends and around the entire high school playground. I saw my peers playing, talking, eating, and laughing, whilst feeling nothing other than liberation.

An eternity passed when I completed the trip and saw the former bully, still lying on the ground with his friends still frozen. His eight months of terror had almost come to an end and with one final outburst of rage, the beast landed the top of his powerful right foot in to the soft meat of the bully's body. The beast had become my enemy. He had betrayed me and had become what I had feared all my young life. He had to let me hug the former bully, now a younger student with his own group of friends who would never make eye contact with me again and I now lived in fear of me with nothing left but disgust with what I had become.

Now almost 188 cm and 80 kg, I had to keep this creature away from people, and so from that day on, I confined myself to a piano at the music centre, the library, or a toilet cubicle.

EDDIE's Return

Distant acquaintances of my parents sent them a card, inviting them and their two boys to the wedding of their daughter. The pre-wedding celebrations were at their home, and it was a delight to be a full head and shoulders above the guests. I was drawn to the living room, where I kept my eyes to the floor as I sat on the corner sofa and listened to the sweet voices of girls my age, memorising the non-sensical conversations they were having with each other as well as with the guys entering the room. Becoming more at ease with being in the midst of people, my eyes would wander, but not to the girls; not yet.

Still observing the room while still seated was when Eddie entered. Not one person flinched as he wandered through.

The joyous atmosphere left no time for anger or anxiety, as he ventured closer.

I noticed that upon standing up, that I had to look down. Way down. Was I ever that short? He was so polite and calm. Two images, one before me and one in my mind; side by side comparing the mighty giant of old and the fat, little man before me.

The object of my rage no longer existed. I tried, but placing my anger I could not.

Perhaps I did deserve to be beaten up back then.

My desire to continue martial arts was all but gone following the wedding.

As fast as the rage entered that day all those years ago, was as fast as it left that evening; and just like that, it was over.

No more Eddie.

Micah entered high school without issue and, like rewinding time, it was my vicarious chance to go down the right path. Reaching puberty many years before him made us seem as more father and son and our conversations were highly intense, mostly involving debating the existence of free will, evolution, humanity, the existence of God, and our concept of time. Horrified many years earlier at the statement by a teacher that the Bible was full of contradictions, I was now disappointed that I had come to the same conclusion; at that time seeing Paul as the twister of an anti-religious message preached throughout Galilee by a possible moral genius.

Micah was blessed with not caring whether he was at all different from others and even though suicidal Jamiel was almost ready to leave us, knowing he could pass on stories from paths not yet taken by his baby brother was a reason to temporarily remain in existence. I always wonder whether Micah, without the knowledge of his older brother's tragic experiences, may have otherwise deviated from the narrow path on which he remained for years to come.

Autistic programming

Almost a decade since being sent over to Harold, Father Sam needed to see how far I'd come with the piano. Both he and Nathaniel were still taller than me, both of similar appearance, would spend an unusual amount of time asking others about their conditions, and would make others helplessly circle them like satellites. Strange it was that one of these men became a priest while the other a street thug. Remapping human categories now had them based upon character and not what they had become; I began rehearsing every movement and facial expression I could memorise from observing adults such as Father Sam. Hours upon hours of practising before the bedroom mirror had now replaced the martial arts training of old, leaving an older teenaged Jamiel to carefully associate the movements with people in different categories as a guide to assist his future self in social situations.

According to Mum and Dad, Rev Sam was fascinated by my talent unkempt after 3 years of no training, and had asked them if he could add that talent as a fixture at his church. The aged choir sounded like a crowd stepping on bag pipes, but it was when they had all left that a wine filled Father Sam would sing through my music as though a perfectly synchronised keyboard of opera voices. It was on one of these occasions that before heading home to his long-term female friend he would scare me with forced eye contact and say with conviction that the young me could not understand:

'Jamiel, before 30 you will be a millionaire.'

Three seconds of eye contact with another human without un-focusing my gaze was enough, but my non-linear perception of time helped me believe that he saw a future that not I, nor anyone else around me could.

There were two other keyboardists that father Sam forced me to play over; both were pretty bad, but I certainly didn't think it fair to be ordered to wash away the sound of their attempts at music simply because the Father felt I had the talent. One Ball Paul (on account of a prior surgery) built me a beautiful synthesiser, but I still betrayed the Father—keeping my volume at a minimum.

The church hymns were terrible; sounding like musical Christmas cards with dying batteries whilst being thrown off a cliff. It was time to drag these hymns into the present. Chris Brack, a classmate who had completed the whole eight-year course at the conservatory, continued to rant on about how he had never witnessed anyone play the piano with such natural talent, especially after I would copy whatever he would play after watching him play it once. Like a typical autistic, none of this felt like an unusual skill or superpower—it only makes one think that they are being tricked in some way or that people are somehow deficient or just plain stupid.

Father would now invite guests to witness what he called a 'prodigy', and the church was beginning to swell with crowds bringing the parish more money during collection times. Hugs from parishioners made me joyously uncomfortable and unaware of what 'rubbing it in one's face' meant, I would assume that the musicians were so happy that this gift of music could be enjoyed by so many people.

Solos with Father Sam who had the undiscovered voice drawing masses of women to mass, would have a spotlight on me whilst accompanying his solos that guests would attend church just to witness.

Standing tall as a man in his thirties looking over his much younger self, I can see the masses absorbed with Father Sam, a church obviously filled by such a female fan base of his.

Over time, the church was nearing capacity, until it one day overflowed. My face was bursting with a feeling an older self can only describe as joy.

Although without bad intention, the typically human musicians perceived this naïve boy's excitement around so many humans as deliberately condescending, and with no reaction from Father Sam, musicians left . . . one by one. After a while, all that remained was a trio comprising of a man called David on the guitar, his young son on drums, and a woman who played the piano very badly. She was a lovely lady who soon disappeared also.

I hated myself for somehow scaring these musicians away, and finally gathered the courage to tell father that I was leaving. He asked me to come back just one more time. It was this one last visit by me that one of the most expensive keyboards I'd ever seen was out and ready with no one playing it. Father told me it was mine. It was difficult for the 16-year-old to process such a gift from a stranger and without a birthday attached. He asked me to play it at the next Mass and give him feedback on how nice it was.

It was very nice.

'Hit it, James!' was his phrase which, of course, would be uttered never too far behind my back at North East Boys'.

I found it strange that David the guitarist would not want to be part of any photo that was taken by a fan after each Mass, with absolutely no idea how increasingly uncomfortable he was with the shifting balance of favouritism. Asked to play at weddings and birthday parties, David would decline when I would ask him to come along; it would be so much better with the three of us!

Father Sam would yell out 'Jami-YEL' before each Mass while the church was still empty and brilliant enough to notice my lack of interest in regular conversations or eye contact, he treated me as an equal.

Not long after, David and his son seemed to start each hymn by counting to two instead of three which seemed an innocent mistake. His troubles increased over the weeks when he consistently played each hymn in the wrong key, or not in the way that I had rewritten it at Father Sam's request. I enjoyed the challenge of keeping on his tail as to appear as though I was aware of any change prior to it occurring. His bizarre behaviour continued for weeks and I just assumed he was trying his best with no second thought, until the day an unusually appreciative fan came up to me as the crowds were departing for the day:

'That was great playing,' said the nice old lady while asking me for a hug and exclaiming that she hoped I never left the church.

'That *was* great playing,' said David with a smile on his mouth that was not mimicked by his eyes, with the accent placed on the 'was' as opposed to the 'great'. Completely thrown off by the behaviour I could not follow left me bewildered until he said the following at my apparent look of confusion. 'You were so loud I couldn't hear myself sing,' he said with what I initially thought to be a smile, but then realising was a slight frown. His eyebrows pointed slightly inward and downwards, which was off his usual eyebrow positioning. Not yet understanding sarcasm, I remained silent after what I thought must have been a compliment.

It was then that the daggers of putrid venom I thought were left behind with the bullies of old were shot forth from him as he looked at me over the rims of his glasses on the end of his nose. I knew this look that was shared so often by bullying teachers who had gotten away with the way they treated my younger self. It was utterly humiliating to have felt protected by a man who then turned out to be enemy attacking. Having no idea how these accusations had any basis in reality, all David was successful in doing was setting off a chain of videos in my head of the abuse heaped upon me by others before him; they were back before me, between us and the effigy of the crucified Christ forever bleeding before the congregation. *Please get me out of this nightmare and back to the darkness where I was not a sickness to be mistreated.* I now hated this place, and I hated him. The beast began to take hold; David wasn't in my age group, he didn't go to school with me, he wasn't related to me, and he was an adult. This could not be happening and I knew that receding into myself would let the beast roam free, but like a floor giving way beneath you, my soul was snatched away by the abyss. Only the beast remained.

I begged the beast to plead with David to get away from me so I could leave the church. He didn't listen and picked up my shaking hand which then turned into a fist:

'You have ten seconds to get away from me before I punch you in the mother-f*****G HEAD.'

My mother always said to allow ten seconds to calm down, so the beast at least gave me that. I was no longer there to restrain him. Adrenalin was pumping. Time was slowing down. Father Sam came out and asked what was going on, which led David to make the worst possible move; he lied.

'Jamiel is threatening me and I didn't do anything,' lied David with such calmness that sent the 16-year-old out of control.

'YOU M****R-F*****G piece of shit. . .' I lunged at him whilst 6' 4" (191 cm) Father Sam came between us like the Berlin Wall. My thin, muscular frame beat on this solid wall, while the beast roared with an anger that must have penetrated David's bones. My mind that had now been annexed entirely by the beast succumbed to a vile rage, wanting to remove the lies and hypocrisy from this place of supposed worship.

'Jamiel, just leave it,' said Father Sam with pure equanimity—it was too much; the sheer forest green of the carpet, the smell of the Church, Father Sam's raised chin, the mother of twins that would belt me at school who was sitting behind me. During an instant of clarity and with insurmountable strength, I climbed out of the abyss to tear both myself and the beast away from the great Christian show and out into the cold.

Mum was horrified by the story and ordered me to apologise as soon as the church opened the next day, whereas my dead grandfather's baby brother on vacation down under was proud that I'd stood up to the manipulative guitarist.

Father Sam had once instructed me to move back to the white mountains north of the holy land as soon as possible and now with Dad's uncle Randy in support of the church tantrum, the answer was simple; I had simply spent my life in the wrong country.

I found Father Sam in the sacristy where the light would stream through the frosted windows of an afternoon, giving a great warmth to the small room adjacent the cold room filled with bleeding Jesus. Not very articulate and still without making eye contact, a mum-inspired mess of an apology was cut off before it could be finished: 'Don't apologise. David has already spoken to me. He said "it's either Jamie or me—I'm not staying if he does" and I told him that Jamiel was not leaving.'

What Father Sam did then was something no one had done before nor since. A precious memory that I share with you almost two decades later from the silence of New Year's Day in the cold, green and white mountains high above my father's birthplace, away from people where the blue sky is both below and above, and in the midst of a perfectly blue sky after last night's snow storm . . . I might stop here for a few minutes.

The final stretch of high school was upon us, and the same guy who liked to ask me to quote verses from the Bible was handing out invitations to his birthday until I approached—but resumed when I had passed. I then walked backwards until close enough again to see him, once again, hold the invites to his chest. That was fun whilst still hurting my younger self's scarred heart from years of stabbing by these so-called peers. It dawned upon me that he wasn't being friendly those years ago when asking for the biblical quotes, but still having no idea what his motive could have been to ask.

I left a note on the kitchen bench for Mum:

> 'I am in a room with no doors and no windows; no
> matter how much I scream I cannot get out.'

My father responded with concern the following afternoon: 'This iz verrry serious my son—why do you wrrrite somesing like zis? Are you trrrying to upset yurrr muzerr?'

She wrote me a letter saying she couldn't talk to me and didn't know how to relate to me but was writing in the hope that we might connect. She worked long hours and had my respect as one would respect a successful business person who rose from obscurity. Taking time off work, she would not refrain from pursuing a cure for her son's acne-infested face. The pill that worked had me bleeding from the nose, mouth, and lower legs—but it decimated the acne to leave a face almost unrecognisable; an almost femininely beautiful face but for the prominent jaw line with thick, dark brown hair that was now even darker with this thing called 'gel' in it. I had finally discovered what had made other school kids' hair look so wet for so long. These looks were undeserved of me.

It was now time to hide my spontaneous outbursts in class by shaking my leg, squeezing my jaw tight, and waiting till the hours of recess to burst out with the syllables in remote parts of the school yard. Dad was worried about my bouts of swear spasms and so was I. Asking Micah to record my actions on video in the hope it would shock me out of the habit backfired as I now knew how ridiculous I would be looking when the uncontrollable outbursts continued.

Now migrating to the edge of the ever more violent Greenacre, Dad's uncle Randy was to stay with us at this proud evidence of his nephew's success. Still not leaving the house without my mountain bike, we ended up at the bastion of Sydney's brilliance where Mum walked Uncle Randy around the Opera house. Bored to tears, I carried my bike up to the top of the steps. With a great breath in while taking in the view of the beautiful city filled with people, I pedalled down the stairs. I would have realised that gravity would be increasing my speed if the stairs were a ramp, but being stairs, this somehow evaded my observations as my bike smashed the stairs head on, forcing me to copy a batman cartoon and close my eyes.

It was like being ejected from a blender as the feeling of stairs disappeared while my bike galloped over more and more steps at once, only to crash into the 5th or 6th step which would then send both me and my bike back into the skies above the Opera House steps. I'm surprised that the handle bars didn't smash into my teenage chin, or that my heart didn't slam into the back of my teeth.

As violent as this process quickly became was as quickly as it subsided when my spooked bike calmed immediately down on the flat surface below the steps; allowing me to open my eyes into a crowd of tourists taking photos of me.

'You're lucky I'm not arresting you, son,' said the kind older gentleman dressed in a blue uniform. Why he would want to arrest a teenager who was convinced that it was gravity's fault was very confusing to the testosterone filled Jamiel.

Mum was furious but Uncle Randy was smiling, only confirming that I was certainly in the wrong country. I told him how glad I was that he'd come to stay, giving me hope when I didn't have any.

Uncle Randy departed home for his children not long after, with a now 17-year-old Jamiel counting down the days until his new life away from his country of birth at school's end; 364 days to go and counting.

Two hundred ninety days to go and I was assigned the arranging of the hymns for the Year 12 graduation Mass. Two hundred days to go and news spread throughout the grade that the reworked hymns were sounding amazing. Ninety days to go and I had achieved my young life's goal. Friends; for a few minutes while leading the blast of sacrilegiously addictive bass, beats, and electricity throughout the school chapel, I now knew that it would mean nothing to my classmates afterwards—but for those few minutes, there was pure elation.

The formal
(The last days)

The chocolate-skinned Hoshanna was three years younger than me, with her striking skin gifted to her by her Arabic ancestors who had joined the Maronite peoples in the recent past.

My brother and I, using data extrapolated over the past few family interactions, were convinced of her interest in me. She responded that she'd love to be my partner for the evening of my year 12 formal, which meant that I could save a distant cousin from the burden.

Composing a song specifically for the occasion brought with it hope for a beautiful evening. The song was to be sung by the school's vice captain who had a good voice, and social skills I'd been mimicking for a while.

The pale-faced 17-year-old Jamiel in a suit was no match for Hoshanna in her long, strapless, blood red dress with her thick, black hair pulled away from her Arabic eyes and blood red lips against her glistening skin. Nathaniel was back in an aggressively restrained sports saloon. The night beginning my new life was set with guys pretending to be lifelong friends with an awkward 17-year-old, a potential girlfriend, and counting the amount of times different people would be entering and departing into the foyer just behind me. It was 9.00 p.m. over the creamy seafood and salad being eaten by the guys and girls chatting away with each other when one sentence from Hoshanna changed the evening: 'It's never going to happen between us.' The child froze as though in an elevator with its cables cut, the sudden shift in weight ripping his insides out his mouth. I am watching him, watching himself from outside his body as Hoshanna commented on the beautifully green eyes possessed by big-nosed Andre. He continued to watch the evening from a distance, and with no sense of self, he advised Andre of Hoshanna's thoughts about his emerald eyes before being handed a drink at the table of his classmates who were very kind to him that evening.

The performance of my composition brought us a standing ovation of overexcited students. This was their night, and their joy let me live another day.

Too many conversations; I could hear every one of them, and wherever I walked, there were more. My mind was counting the number of drinks being served, the number of tables in the room, the number of seats per table, which tables had more seats due to social connections, the number of teachers and which teachers were there and which students they chat to. Never would this guy be accepted amongst these crowds, and through the thick atmosphere of conversations, music, and running waiters, I could see the alternative crowd from the music centre. So comfortable did they seem with both drinking and drugs, it was finally time to test this body with a shot of vodka.

They were so nice to me which almost brought me to tears as they welcomed me to their table. Offered a jug of beer by my evening's protectors, they explained to me what a 'skol' was before I invited the whole jug into my bloodstream. 'Are you okay?' asked the very likeable college prefect who had talentedly blown away the chapel with his drumming to my rewritten church hymns.

'*Of course,*' I now knew how to respond to basic questions with short answers.

Needing to check on Hoshanna at this point, I stood up and walked into the carpeted wall. Wait . . . the walls were not carpeted. Somehow they now shared the same carpet as the floor. *Why is the floor the wall?*

I hadn't eaten since 1.20 p.m. that day.

Only islands of two-second videos can be remembered from that point on; Hoshanna sitting alone at her table, Hoshanna dancing whilst holding her handbag with indeterminate facial expressions, Jamiel raising his long arms high at the deputy headmaster, and a completely unexpected hug from long lost Jonathan while I kept my arms by my side in the same foyer that I couldn't figure out why so many guys and girls wanted to keep visiting.

After Jonathon, the second hug in many years came from Mum when I got home. Too much human contact for an evening concluded with a 17-year-old Jamiel crying for the first and last time that I can remember. 'I hate her,' I said over and over. Mum shut Dad up as he yelled from the other side of their bed: 'Stoop huggin' heem. Boot him too bed. Tell him stobba swerrrin.'

Ten days to go while I sat against a wall upstairs and looking out the window without moving, counting the amount of times the trees would sway in the wind with each passing hour. From seemingly nowhere on the seventh day, John's older sister Jenny called for me: 'You're leaving in a few days. You have your whole life ahead of you—get over it and move on.' *You're right*, I thought.

And so I did.

PART 2

Jamiel had been driving me out of Sydney for quite a while now, but the guy behind the wheel was now someone I had no idea until now was a child with the face of a man. He should not be so calm after such a life. I lose my **** if I'm not fed on time and here is this guy who has every reason to become a psycho serial killer or one of those nut jobs you hear about on the dinner-time news. This was not the best thought to have when looking around and seeing no signs of life.

'Is my story boring you, Renn?'

'Um . . . no. So what kind of ladies did you meet in Lebanon? If it's anything like Turkey, then I'm sure your younger self is about to have a great time over there.'

The timing couldn't have been better as the car had stopped as I watched Jamiel stroll to the hotel lobby whilst requesting I follow.

'I will be back tomorrow with some clothes and a car for you from Sabrina.'

Here I was, wanting to be at a home that didn't exist with no phone, no spare clothes, ID, or money.

'The four of us have organised room service for you, along with a private room for you to be safe in for now. Don't leave that room in the unlikely event that one of your mother's crazy connections has somehow followed us here. It makes sense that they would be looking for you all night now. You are the only one who can testify against the illegal activities your mother is involved in now.'

How the hell did he know about that. . .

'Maths' as he turned around on his way back to his long drive home.

The next day just had me watching TV, dumbing my thoughts, delaying facing any drama awaiting me outside that climate-controlled room with a great room service menu and mini-bar. I may have missed Turkey's lifestyle, but this came pretty close. The day was almost complete before it was tarnished by a phone call from Jamiel, who said he wasn't able to come today but for me to enjoy the holiday and he would do everything in his power to ensure he was there tomorrow. He asked me not to take any other calls for the evening.

Still with my TV marathon well after the sun went down, I must have fallen asleep to the pitch black outside this island of a room in a hotel in the middle of nowhere.

I was awoken to a concierge advising me that the gentleman that had dropped me off was outside and that some clothes were on their way to my room.

Of course, it was Jamiel:

'One of the phrases I've learned to ask is—How are you feeling?'

I felt . . . I wasn't sure how I was feeling. I was definitely scared at the very least. Maybe being locked away was better; at least I had clothes and a fake family.

'Sabrina's old car has been sitting around since I made her enough money to get the beauty you have wished was yours for quite a while.'

'Thanks Jamiel.' Once again, he was about to miss out on a serving of sarcasm.

'No need to thank me, Renn. Sabrina did a great thing here and I look forward to the day that your success can pay her back.'

I looked forward to the day Jamiel would get sarcasm. When this was all over, I promised that I would teach him that.

'Would you like to know why I had to delay meeting you?'

I actually wasn't that interested until he placed his smart phone underneath my nose. The picture of a mashed up face smothered in blood was horrific to watch but was made infinitely worse when I recognised who it was.

'This is what your mother's men did to my brother yesterday, Adrienne. We were both in hospital, but I got out early to be here with Sabrina's gifts.' I didn't realise that he had been injured in any way until he removed his glasses at the end of that sentence, revealing an eye floating in a sea of blood and purple pus.

'Jamiel, I am so sorry!'

'There is no need to be sorry, Renn. It was not your fault, but don't let my brother's broken cheekbone be in vain. Tell the truth when we get to where we are going.'

I thought I was driving to a safe house.

'After speaking with Eleina and Sabrina, I was advised to travel with you to the edge of the state where a very bright, female police officer is very interested in taking down your story. At that point, you can decide whether to keep going interstate or trying to rebuild your life with the support of NSW Social Services.

'How about you, Jamiel? What will you do?'

'I plan to tell you the rest of my story. It's going to be a long trip. Hopefully by then, both my face and Micah's cheekbone and eye socket will be on their way to recovery after our date with Toupee and his jelly-bellied, testosterone-filled sidekick.'

'Did you at least call the police, Jamiel?'

'I did. The officer was a very nice man who asked me whether I was able to get the licence plate of the car type assailants came in.'

'Well, did you get it or not?'

'I handed it to the policeman, explaining that I was only able to rip off the back one.'

'You gave him the actual licence plate?'

'What do you mean? Was I supposed to give him a fake one?'

1998
Freedom

It felt like being on the other side of suicide when boarding the Gulf Air flight for the near east. The pain of my existence did not enter the plane, and it slowly faded from view as we climbed higher and higher, away from the wrong country and into an afternoon that took a great time to fade into night.

I got along very well with the 4-year-old Somali boy during the first leg. He understood my limited Levantine-Arabic and I thought I understood his African-Arabic in return, until he asked me if I was a

Halal Muslim. I had been officially studying the Quran and the Arabic script for a few months during free classes now and was absorbed in the ideology that had been kept so separate but so close for so many centuries. What Maronites around the world had grown up to believe were pockets of Islamic no-go zones in a western country, were trying to be seen by Jamiel as an Arabic culture native to Lebanon itself; a heretical thought to the Maronites of old. After counting whatever I could on that plane ride, I turned to the unending sand below us roll out for what seemed like hours; fixating on the road which sliced opened the earth below like a knife, exposing the darkness of Arabia beneath the hot sand.

While thinking this, the road became slightly blurry. I blinked, thinking I had maybe become even more blind, until it became clear again, followed by more blur. They were clouds interrupting my view of the road below until my view was washed out, throwing me back into my seat from the sheer brightness of the white world, but I didn't need to adjust for long.

Within moments, the sea of white was defeated by a sea of shimmering blue: the Mediterranean Sea.

Never had I seen such an achingly beautiful scene in my short life; as though Botany Bay and the Blue Mountains had collided, leaving Sydney squashed and on a forty-five-degree angle. High rises surrounded by blue seas on one side and majestic green mountains on the other, getting larger and larger until the shudder of high speed winds engulfed our cabin as our Jet touched down between the shimmering blue on one side and the green giants on the other. The herd of passengers cheered around me as though it were New Year's Day. I had arrived.

'They are going to see me all grown up for the first time,' I was telling myself, 'they will see how much I've changed and I'm sure they will love what I have become.' Pushing my luggage on the trolley towards the closed doors that would soon open for me onto a crowd of family members, I took in a deep breath. The doors opened out to an ocean of foreigners and I heard cheering. Gradually, the crowd began to dissipate with the now very familiar rate of exponential decrease that had become so synonymous with human nature to my young mind, leaving me almost completely alone to trample back and forth over the marble floors while hearing regular announcements in both French and Arabic over the P.A. system.

None of that cheering was for Jamiel. None of his family appeared to be anywhere to be found.

Perhaps at the wrong airport, I spent two and a half hours travelling between the taxi stand, the public phone, and the men's room. *'Do I take a taxi?''But where do I go? and with what money?'* having not yet paid for anything other than lollies, milk, and newspapers.

I asked what turned out to be a non-native cleaner if she knew how to get to my uncle's place. After describing his glasses and facial features, she shook her head and kept walking.

'I could use the public phone?', but there was nowhere to place any money and I did not know anyone's phone number. Stinking and sweating, I began to prepare a place to sleep for the night.

Two-and-a-half hours later, I was the object of attention for a mass of family members who ordered me to embrace them.

Uncle Randy was shocked, 'Kiss them. What are you waiting for?'

'I waited two and a half hours, Uncle' is what I didn't say.

Still lacking the ability to articulate these thoughts, I put out my hand to shake each of theirs, having no idea how much this would offend them.

I think my family was speaking to me when we were in one of the procession of cars owned by a Levant Family member, but I focused on the picture before me; a vast sea to the left and mountains which rose into the clouds immediately to my right.

A gigantic statue of Jesus, a symbol of a once Christian country, stood at the base of one of the steep-green paths to the clouds. Disorientating to see a city built on such an angle, I remained unable to look away despite it making me nauseous.

After a while on this solid, eight lane highway which I would one day get to speed on, the land around me rotated as we exited off the former runway and began climbing into the sky. Within minutes, I could see the coastal city of Batroun and its bay beneath us as though back on the plane.

The temperature dropped and the air became cooler, sharper, and crisp. Buildings were replaced with centuries old stone houses. Centuries old stone houses then turned into fields of fruits and vegetables, goats, cows and elderly widows I was sure grew up with the horse and carriage throughout their younger days.

Dad's hometown welcomed me with an ear-piercing quiet, allowing hundreds of memories to punch the inside of my skull as loud as ever.

The night brought on a Mediterranean buzz that had teenage me in an erratic state that ran free with no parents or teachers to condemn it. The entire suburb was as though a gigantic café; flocks of people were out socialising with my body overwhelmed with adrenalin that wanted to tear through my skin. The stone wheel that Dad had used before the horse took over was on its side where it had been since before the 6-year-old Jamiel witnessed, in the midst of flying bullets, his dad and grandad pick up the man who had been shot in the neck as he died in their arms. That solid stone wheel was well taller than a human, bigger than a small truck, and wider than a fridge, meaning that Dad must have really had strength at that age that I could not comprehend.

'You've only just got here,' people would say as I walked through their homes from its front entrance to its rear whilst sucking in as much data as I could, where they placed objects and what seemed to be used with greater frequency, what age groups were inside vs the age groups outside, who was whom and why that mattered to me. I assured them I'd be back.

This hyped-up-almost 18-year-old did not calm down as the night aged into twilight; he needed to capture all he could with his camera to share with the world so far away what it was missing. Families were not shy from physical affection which I was not used to witnessing and didn't like to think about.

The cousin who once showed me off as the hot 18-year-old was now more subdued, and I was almost 18. Hoping to share this with her, I burst out with the closest rehearsed line that seemed appropriate:

'Hi Rachel,' I called out, 'you don't have the fire in your bum like you used to.'

'What do you mean?' she queried.

I didn't mean a physical fire burning inside her lower body. It was a metaphor, which went against my nature to use but I believed was the way humans communicated. Perhaps I was wrong. This seemed to terribly upset Rachel, but I calculated that I had at least 15 more cousins

I could try and generate a relationship with; 15 more shots of trial and error. Those odds seemed pretty good at the time.

To practise social techniques before losing an additional cousin, it was time to try again with a group of guys and gals having a chat.

'Hi, how are you,' I said, extending my hand to someone in the group. So far it was going well. With no idea what to do next, I quickly scanned my stored database of movie lines, then launched my conversation starter to the guy speaking within the group at the time.

'My name's Jamiel and I heard you eat shit.' It was now time to pay an ever higher price for being judged simply as not-so-nice neurotypical. In summary, the guy was pissed.

'Give him a break,' one of the girls said, 'he's from Australia. That's probably how they speak over there.' It would be a good idea to let them keep thinking that.

'Look, I've embarrassed myself,' I said, realising that I must have made a mistake. *'That's enough punishment. Let's move on.'*

He never did.

Trying to say the right thing was like trying to carry an egg on a tea-spoon in the black of night.

Why were people getting angry with me merely copying their own lines and body language? Was it the age, the location, my accent, the time of day? Like fresh lava destroying anything in its path, this land was quickly turning into the one from which I had escaped. Family contact decreased, funny looks when simply walking down the street.

'Australians are weird,' as I had seemingly become the ambassador for the country that had exiled me.

Eugene was Uncle Randy's son and lived on society's edge as did I, but what I found strange was that he could delve in to their world as a native at any time of his choosing, only to return home on his time. Why would one want to be where I was out of choice?

With his lectures to me at night, he would teach me how to better behave; how to anticipate other people's reactions, how to deliberately put doubts into their minds about each other and thereby sabotaging relationships of those around him for personal gain.

That part was weird.

According to Eugene, people were both stupid and dangerous and if I didn't learn quickly how to control them then they would destroy me. I really wanted to adopt his mindset as the only way ever presented to me as a cure for being such a disease, but it resulted in a feeling that I can only describe as being in an unlit cathedral, or on train tracks in a tunnel at night while hearing a woman screaming from an indeterminate location. It seemed so clear to me that he took pleasure from—and in—fooling ordinary humans, but there was no one to whom this could be explained. Each family member would cut ties with me over the next few weeks whilst Eugene looked upon refusal to adopt his behaviour with discontent. The days became quieter, and Christmas Eve came with a phone call from Mum back home: 'Be careful . . . you know what you are like in crowds.'

Not understanding what this could mean, I remained quiet if ever in the presence of three or more people.

Not knowing what to do from then on as nights and days spun over the unchanging mountains surrounding the green valley of my new home, I prayed the prison wouldn't encapsulate both my homelands. If God existed, then he had a wicked sense of humour as he answered my prayers as soon as I hung up with him:

'Your dad's on the phone.'

I went inside and picked up the phone.

'You have to cam beck to oustrrralya,' he said.

The young Jamiel clutched onto the phone like a child clutching to his mother's hair.

'I can't,' he said with complete desperation.

'Yes, you will. This iz it.' My father and his accent had spoken; it was final.

My arm had cramped up. Seventeen years of solitary confinement was enough although Dad's older brother, Pretty Boy Henry, had secretly ordered his baby brother to, 'Get your son out of here'—and had also deeply troubled Mum when strongly advising her that I needed help.

Uncle Randy advised me to hug each family member and apologise for reasons unknown to me. He was right as they all forgave me for whatever sins I had supposedly committed against them, and all seemed to be okay.

A birthday boy with orange hair he intended to die blonde and fifteen hours of video footage was back at the organised and quiet city of Sydney when compared to the chaos of the battered and alive, Mediterranean Jewel.

The suicidal young man felt the warm liquid drip ever so carefully from his hazel eyes, down his white face and past his pink lips as he was escorted back to his windowless cell.

Da Nile of my power

High school final results had arrived, which need a little context placing:

Before the high school final exams and before part 1 of his life had concluded, Jamiel's mother had asked him how he had all of a sudden come to read and write classical Arabic, a language unintelligible to the Maronite Arabic speaker not educated in it.

It was then that he explained to her how a baby book left behind by Uncle Randy converted him into a reader and writer of basic classical Arabic within ninety-six hours, going on to read texts during free classes at the school's library.

'Imagine what you could do if you actually did any work,' said Mum as I tried to imagine doing work—not realising that she was looking for a response until she turned that statement into a question.

'Mum, if I can pass by doing almost no work, then that is a gift that must be taken advantage of. There are many people who have to work very hard just to pass and I should not take that for granted.'

Strangely, there is no memory of anything between that statement and Mum's response:

'Jamiel, if you won't do it for you then please give your HSC a serious go for me.'

Painfully opening the advanced maths course that had been dragging me by the knuckles for the past two years, I read it from cover to cover; followed by completing a practice exam. The next day, I attempted the exam only to achieve one of the highest marks in the school grade.

The video stored on my adult brain shows a 40-year-old mother more saddened than outraged when finding out: 'Why didn't you do this from the beginning?!' she asked.

'Never happy, parents are' was the first thing that comes into the teenager's conscious mind.

Curious to see if this strange new gift could be replicated, it was time to read the physics syllabus each day over a two-week period before the exam since I had spent more time out of class than in at the request of my late physics teacher. This time it was the top handful of students in the entire state of NSW that I was now a part of, with the same result in advanced music making it the year's trifecta.

Anyway, the results came in whilst I was failing at a new life in the far away mountains and despite failing all other subjects, Sydney University offered to engineer this boy into an engineer.

'Jami-YEL' as an 18-year-old, Jamiel imitated his role model while awkwardly stepping into an empty church.

I waited for the Father, but apart from my echoes the church remained quiet. Father was nowhere to be found. It was a brain tumour that had him collapse during one of his bible classes whilst I was away. Never compelled to see a human before hearing those echoes in the empty church, I had to know in which hospital he was residing.

Conversations hurtling past me as I counted how many patients in each room had visitors and how many visitors per patient were speaking and what age. Mum had me take chocolates which I nervously handed the bald Father through his female friend. Trying to recognise the Father's facial expressions were even more difficult without both his eyebrows and overabundance of wavy grey hair that women of the church had once seemed to notice as he mentioned being fine whilst quickly asking about my family. He was good at that. Not knowing how long to stay in the room, I grew nervous after counting over 100 seconds, and left within minutes. He said he was recovering which had to make sense since he was aged well below the average adult male at death as per Mum's statistics book I had read at age 11.

As the desire to resume the new-found life discovered in the northern hemisphere outgrew the space available under Mum and Dad's roof, it was time to try my young hand at employment; cleaning toilet floors and ashtrays of gambling smokers. Being around people for such a ridiculous amount of time, brought on a disturbing level of discomfort that by now had to be fought by the 18 year old as he struggled through the 11.00 p.m. to 7.00 a.m. shift at a pay rate that was almost triple what one would expect to earn at that age.

Some new rules discovered included the following:

- Don't rub a man's pants after dropping beer on them.
- Avoid the staff member who asks you whether your lips are so pink from eating p***y.
- Answer 'good' when someone asks, 'How are you?' but then ask them how they are back.
- Make sure your feet point in the direction that you wish to walk.
- Not everyone who asks you how you are is actually a nice person.

Twenty weekends of the above, and it was time to resign and wish a very begrudging Mum and Dad a farewell, but not before Mum made me accept her gift of $250 in spending money.

The hitchhiker

Never having been back at Dad's homeland during the summer, I didn't expect the thirty-three degrees when Uncle Randy advised to me to take only limited items into the mountains for a few days. With the thirty-three-degree heat now set to twenty-five at the new altitude, Uncle Randy handed me some bread, meat, and cheese, telling me he had 'some things to do'.

Not knowing when Uncle Randy would be back, I rationed the food he'd left me in the old underground olive press which kept me cool as I fed on the bread and a slice of raw onion. Each day was spent waiting for Uncle Randy to return.

Days later saw me run out of the meat and cheese, while I sat on the balcony's swing bed as each day passed, counting the number of times per minute I would swing back and forth whilst counting the vehicles that passed through the valley. *'I reckon I could jump in one of these cars.'* Half a month later and I was now so hungry that I gave up waiting for Uncle's return, standing at the side of the road until a little red van stopped next to me. The gentle, red-headed man asked where I was going.

'I don't know, but I've always wanted to see more of the country.' Through the delivery driver, I visited tiny villages sprinkled through much higher altitudes and temperatures that began to feel like a restaurant cool room. Each breath was like a mouthful of mints, and the higher we rose, the nicer the people. The mountains overlooking Dad's old home were black upon my return, and the next day I knew I had to go farther.

Further and further I hiked, memorising the conversation starters that worked best with each adventure until the day I had the chance to hike higher than the clouds themselves to a land from a story book.

Its name was Bet-Haven and was the city of Mum's birth; filled with the eastern European version of the Scottish Stereotype you may have seen in some Hollywood flicks.

An overtly Catholic city, I first felt its reputation when my Arabic driver would only drop me off at the town's border, not daring to enter. A bizarre concept upon witnessing this, I hopped out and used the energy of an ice cream to walk the thirty minutes needed until reaching the town's centre near the violent waterfall from which fountains were fuelled. Higher than the highest peaks of our beautiful Australian Snowy Mountains, I was surrounded by snow that rose more than twice as high as Bet-Haven itself, which formed a gigantic crescent around the edge of a gaping abyss that only Bet-Haven's inhabitants would built homes right up to. This gaping 'hole' in the earth would often be filled with clouds while also an escape for the powerful waterfalls to vanish in to.

Soon learning the history of this ancient town to be filled with the Mediterranean's earliest inhabitants who had survived every local invasion in human history, I could then understand their apparently 'tough' nature, and strange but loveable accent; both of which I did not expect from such fair-skinned, European looking people.

Distant relatives of Mum's allowed me a break from living on bread and onions. Freshly cooked meat, fruits and fresh attention brought with it new-found strength and inspiration; and with that it was time to face Uncle Randy at his home way down on the boiling hot coast.

Within an hour, the temperature blasted back at me with thirty-eight-degree heat as I stepped out of the kind driver's car and into the heat from which the sweat on my skin would not evaporate into. Feeling as though covered with melted wax, I impatiently knocked on Uncle Randy's front door. His wife, and Eugene's mother, answered the door.

'Why did Uncle leave me there? What happened—I thought he must have been dead!' not aware that my voice was raised.

Uncle Randy appeared from the shadows, 'GaaBY, I'll take it that you yell at me but I refuse to accept you shouting at my wife.' Remaining silent, he continued, 'You are an embarrassment to the family.'

The exile to the village must have been deliberate.

Standing outside at Uncle Randy's request, not knowing what was going on, I had no understanding outside of the meaning of each word from of each sentence spoken to me. This somehow also angered Uncle Randy even further.

Without understanding the sudden turn to aggression, I did nothing as Uncle Randy punched me in the face then closing the door. Stung and confused, I sat on the steps as I parted ways with the illusion of family bestowed upon my 6-year-old self all those years ago.

Catching a taxi half-way up the mountains with the little change from Mum I had left, I continued to where people were scarce and where the mountains remained unchanged.

So many adventures and the culture of this still European Country was becoming so apparent with the more drivers I would meet from Arab lands across the border, separated by the Great River.

Was it great in size, in stature, or in popularity? What did the Arab lands look like over the other side? I had to set off at sunrise.

Hours of traversing mountains and valleys past both clouds and rivers, less and less life was being seen. The tall, blonde soldier ordered me to 'take care, and be careful', as he disappeared behind the bus into the heat and dust after sharing the first half of the bus ride with me towards the horizon.

Walking towards the border through what seemed to be kids of African descent playing in the dust, I grabbed a coke from a fridge that was plugged in to a generator with nothing else around it but for a house with no walls, windows, or doors; exactly the opposite of what I had been encased within my whole life. Not far from the dust, I had finally caught up with the horizon; it was a three-metre-high wall with a ladder against it. I was so excited to have reached the end of this world and the beginning of the Arab lands. Once the very old Gypsies had cleared from my path up the ladder, I fought my phobia of heights and disappeared over the wall.

The 'Great River'

All I could see was a crappy little polluted creek with an obviously Arabic-looking man sitting alone on a deck chair.

'So this is the great river, is it?' I asked, sitting on the ground next to his chair. It seemed the horizon wasn't that interesting. Hot and tired, it was time to go back home disappointed.

Leaping out of his deck chair, the Saddam Hussein lookalike grabbed me by the waist and pushed me back on to the ground before pulling out his handgun and placing it at my right ear.

'You're not going anywhere. What are you doing here?'

'I just came to see the river.' I told him without thinking anything untoward.

'Who are you and where do you come from?' He had a lot of questions for me, but he seemed quite nice despite his eagerness to keep me next to his beach chair.

'I could kill you right now,' he said while not lowering his gun. He then asked to see my ID, and I quickly whipped out my trusty Australian driver's licence.

'How do I know this is not a fake?' he asked. This was when I began to grow very nervous. Taking my wallet from me, he saw what remained of my mother's gift to me before leaving her home.

'Did you know that US dollars are illegal here?' he asked me.

'They are not illegal over that wall,' as I expressed my wish to go home in the midst of him laughing at my apparent joke.

'How do I know you are not an Israeli spy,' he asked me, 'your Arabic is very bad.'

I responded, 'If I were a spy, I am definitely not a very good one.'

'Im just a kid who goes from school to church to home,' responding before he then asked me to quickly shut my mouth and play along while he put his handgun away. I did not know I was in a game, but I definitely didn't like it.

A very dark and slender man of almost Indian appearance appeared out of the grass with a massive automatic rifle pointed straight at me until it was between my eyes. As instructed, I kept playing the 'mouth shut' game while he asked my new friend in the deck chair who I was.

'Nobody. Just a friend from over the wall coming to visit,' he said. With the automatic weapon at my face, it was my turn to answer the same question. I could feel a drop of sweat drip from my little finger while hoping my response did not expose my supposedly bad Arabic. *'His friend,'* popped out and lingered between us along with the rifle for a few more torturous seconds, before he commenced a brief but heated conversation in Syrian with my new friend, before vanishing into the thick grass.

'You're lucky I pulled you over; look up there.' I looked up to where my friend was pointing and in the distance saw the road to what seemed a more official border with a stream of traffic passing through.

'Had you gone through there, you would have disappeared.'

He said he didn't take bribes but as a gesture of thanks he asked me to give him something whilst pointing at my wallet. He refused to take the American dollars.

My now lighter wallet and I quickly escaped back over the wall to find what looked like a spirited man possessing the familiar, European dialect with a scattering of French words. I was with one of my own. He was incredulous after hearing the story, saying I was the first person he'd heard of who'd come back alive, and the first Christian at the very least. Logic suggested that the wall was perhaps more likely for Syrians escaping Arab lands than the other way around. My Syrian friend and his deck chair must have been making quite a living collecting 'tolls'. Tomorrow I would head in the opposite direction in the hopes of visiting the sick Father's beloved holy land. This time I'd be more careful of walls.

Standing of a cool evening in a neighbouring town square wearing a suit and thongs, I was quoting facts and figures to the seemingly interested group of girls who would not cease asking me about Australia.

The three popular guys, owning pointless objects such as new cars, new clothes, and new phones, made my night even more euphoric by befriending me. As though finally cast a role in a movie, the rear door of a BMW opened with Antony beckoning me into the car.

'Hey, how are you?' continuing my social interactive experiment. I tried again as we drove into the black.

'How are you?' I repeated.

'Good, you f*****g b*****d,' said Thomas.

Maintaining my grin from ear to ear with my new-found friends, Thomas turned around.

'Didn't you hear me—you're a f*****g idiot. Stay away from my girls.'

The North East boys missed out on my friendship, but I was now popular and therefore remained smiling. 'It's not a f*****g joke and don't let me see you with the girls again.'

It was quite cold where they had dropped me off with the light of the moon streaming through trees. Not long before beginning the trek back over the mountains, a very short guy nicknamed 'Tall guy' gave me a lift back in his delivery truck. His driving was totally reckless, one day eventually ploughing both him and his Mercedes down a flight of stairs and into a church wall on a Sunday.

I felt great and almost called out 'hey' when the popular guys came to visit me of an evening born not long thereafter, before Thomas dangled his middle finger back and forth whilst cruising past me and my family with his entourage. Eugene's sister Rose calmed me with sweet words whilst Uncle 'Pretty-Boy' Henry's daughter Mariah edged on my rage.

This can't be happening on the other side of the world. A sea of rats crawled into the scene carrying with them nothing but disgust, embarrassment, and a rage I had never known.

I needed to be alone and sat perched at the end of the street, thinking about the one promise I broke by reading a Gospel only 2.5 times and not the three that Father Sam had asked the congregation to do so many years before.

It was now almost twilight when Rose and Mariah were still arguing; one grateful that I had remained composed whilst the other wishing an alternate ending of vengeance. My sadness was interrupted when a black BMW passed through the town centre only to turn around and stop a few metres away, while a second nice car edged ever nearer to the three of us with each passing moment. It was Thomas yelling for me to 'get in.'

Rose begged me not to go, while Mariah still wanted revenge. Wherever it was, I wanted home.

'No worries, man,' was a new saying that fit perfectly while I moved towards the back door while wondering whether to repeat the same mistake. My hands were shaking while I whispered an apology to Rose before I took a deep breath, wrenching open the driver's door. There was no beast this time, just me.

Thomas didn't see my right fist as it collided with his mouth and after losing a tooth, he backed desperately away from the unrelenting punches and into his friend's lap as I kneeled onto the driver's seat. Now in the driver's seat and continuing Mariah's vengeance and Rose's disappointment against the sorry Thomas, the car began to roll backwards with increasing speed as we were carried down the hill. Had I not been so engrossed in a childish need for vengeance, I may have noticed a metre-deep gutter for the melting winter snows; but like an elevator free falling with gravity we fell into it, then smashing into the side of Uncle Randy's house. Having rested my left shin on the side of the car for easy punching, the impact brought car metal into my lower knee, releasing a sea of blood I would not feel for quite a while.

Rose and her mother hid me in the underground cavern with the remaining onions while an inter-village dispute ensued. It turned out that the boys were descended from the very same woman who had given birth to the girl that would eventually die giving birth to Baby Dad.

Never would I desire physical violence again.

Rachel's bike was beautiful, and it was worth descending to the coast to be one with it in freedom along the lagoon-coloured sea between the world's oldest cities. Attempting to use it to escape to the mountains for good, it took almost two hours to climb half a kilometre. The position of the sun made it clear that I would not make it before the hyenas came out to play, with no choice but to turn around and gain a speed I had never reached through pedalling alone. Overtaking a vehicle at highway speeds disallowed the naïve teenager to anticipate the gravel-filled corner which would soon render his steering useless. The bike skidded towards the metre-high concrete barrier overlooking the 500-metre drop, and it was finally time to be dragged towards my own extinction.

The bike was crushed against the barrier with momentum grabbing me by the shoulders and throwing me over the cliff's edge.

Oh, shit, I'm going to die!

I flew over and heard complete silence.

Any fear remained at the concrete barrier, leaving me with nothing but peaceful acceptance of my own demise.

As I flew through the air, I took in the beautiful view of the shimmering blue sea and the hundreds of buildings below, never feeling so calm as I dived into the inevitable.

Then I blacked out.

It was a tree growing out of the cliff that saved me. Climbing the fifteen metres back up the cliff, I was greeted with anxious faces outside countless open car doors, people asking if I was okay. I asked the crowd why they kept asking this question until one man asked me to look down at my blood-covered arms and legs, with a long and deep gash in one leg as a bonus. Gladly accepting the tissues and saying goodbye to the crowd, I picked up the bike with its now square-shaped tyres, allowing gravity to take the buckled mess back to the coast where Eugene looked at me like I was crazy.

'You are crazy,' he said with a combination of tones too difficult to process at the time, 'Truly there is something wrong with you.' Rachel took the bike as I promised to buy her a new one while she closed the door behind both her and the wreckage. No longer did I fear death. No more was the fear of the cell and I rejoiced in the epiphany that no other could see. Now fearless against the dark spirit of depression and anxiety, it was time to leave the wreckage of what I hoped would be a new life, and return home.

BE LIKE THE FIRST FIVE MINUTES

Using my last $50 to buy $5 ice creams once per day, fighting off the hunger between the days that Uncle Pretty Boy's wife offered me some baked beans of an evening with some bread.

The youngest of Dad's few cousins was just about to start a new life in New York as he took me to the airport in his classic MG. 'What a Wonderful World' burst from its speakers as it mixed with the glimmering sea at speed. Pulling up to the departure area while leaving the car running, he spoke to me.

'When you arrived, we thought you were great; then for some reason, you would change into something we couldn't understand. Just be that person you were for the first five minutes from now on, and then maybe your luck will change for the better.'

I would begin timing the first five minutes of each future encounter with another person from then on.

The red sun was getting ready to sink below the blue sea for the last time, as I watched the MG speed off into the distance.

Believe it or not, I actually saw the old Baptist pastor at the airport after not seeing him and his followers for so long. He didn't seem to recognise me with my taped-together glasses—I had to keep testing them after the optician had told me how durable they were—and a ponytail I had forced my stubbornly thick hair into.

Mum felt a new level of pain when seeing her son whom had lost almost 20 per cent of his body mass.

What goes around comes around

Suicide was no longer an act of which to be ashamed, but a sign of strength against the army of severe depression. I was getting closer to the final act and looked forward to the right time as a 19-year-old Jamiel spent his days in the corner of his black room, only inches away from pure grief and hopelessness.

Unbeknownst to anyone, brother Micah who had hit puberty during his time as an only child had been weight training each day in the black before sunrise for eighteen months, leaving me returning to his recognisable baby face on an unrecognisable body of pure muscle with wrists, a neck and shoulders that could tackle a bull. During a rare day of ceasefire by Depression's army, a boy dressed as a gangster rapper squeezed his shoulder against Micah's elbow when we were out at the shopping centre whilst mum and dad shopped for necessities. The younger boy of Pacific Islander extraction but dressed as an American

Hip-Hop producer was confusing to me, but what wasn't confusing to me was how he was asking my gigantic little brother for the time. I had seen enough movies to know what the plan of this young boy was. Warning Micah many times not to wear his graduation gift of jewellery from Mum and Dad if we were to ever walk in public, I pulled him away with frustration as innocent Micah raised his wrist to look at his watch. This was a set up. I grabbed Micah with a degree of aggression that his poor baby face did not understand, but he did understand the slashing movement that the young punk made across his throat whilst failing before running off.

I knew this wasn't a joke.

'Run . . . back into the shopping mall . . . right now,' I told Micah. The main mall was filled with people shopping and I felt safe before a large guy put his arm around Micah as if he was a long-time friend.

'Who do you think you are, messing with us?' In an instant I was sent to the ground in bewilderment. Through dizziness, I captured the following:

- The young lady in her early thirties simply gazing down at me whilst holding onto the pram holding her baby.
- Six young gangsters surrounding Micah with their punches having no effect upon my passive baby brother's frame.

No longer possessing any desire for violence, I allowed them to hit the body in which I was encased to their hearts content whilst looking at those around us who did nothing but watch. After feeling violent hits to the back of the head a few more times, it was a massive security guard who stomped head on into the gang which scattered like a flock of pigeons, bar one skinny 16-year-old who got a few more kicks in to me before bolting, leaving me with a broken nose and smashed teeth.

When we got back to the car, Dad took one look at me and started screaming—'How dare you let them hit you.'

Although I wanted to explain to this person that I was no longer interested in fighting people and that it happened so quickly that I was still in shock, what came out was 'F*** you'.

The police were quite honest about their futility in this case, but there had to be a better solution other than violence. Since both Micah and the security guard were unharmed with the common factor between them being their size, it was time to commence the same journey. Each day brought with it over two hours of intense training, and by the time my second time around at uni had arrived, it was a larger, ponytailed, crooked nosed, ceramic toothed, rigid upper body, and broad-shouldered stranger that I was glad could now keep me company.

Uni round 2

After the failed attempt at civil engineering twelve months prior at Sydney uni, the newly created bank of conversation starters was ready to be tested when recommencing uni in 2000. I thanked Mum very much for the car she bought to get me to classes fifty kilometres away, with her trusting me when advising her that I would know how to drive a 'manual' before study began. Within an hour—thanks to the impressive explanation from massive Micah on how a manual transmission worked—I could see the picture in total and could now drive manual cars.

Filled with confidence at stepping out of this very old, manual car with my now muscled up frame that didn't yet feel as though it belonged to me, I started with anyone I could find, and before long I had friends— at least what I thought a friend was as per my observations. The rule that others seemed to know was where 'one must not try making friends during lectures'. The lecturer who, arms crossed, had been watching my progress around the room, asked,

'Are you right there?'

I thought it was nice of him to ask me that in front of the students, so I decided to show off my ability to respond to the human question with *'Yes, I'm fine thank you, how about you?'*

Laughter filled the auditorium for a reason I wasn't exactly sure about; first suspecting that I had somehow offended the lecturer when he wouldn't answer my questions in the subsequent tutorial. Post the session, I was approached by students asking how I remained so calm after the tutorial comments which I was not even aware of.

Embarrassed and humiliated, I jumped into the next men's room:

'You are stuck in a grown up's body now, Jamie,' whispering to my reflection in the mirror, 'from the edge of the world and from death itself you have returned, taller, larger, and older than the kid who was abused by the animals.'

'These people can see through the act,' responded my reflection, 'and there is no way that you are any different from what you have been all your life.'

'But what am I?' I asked myself . . . there was no response.

The bathroom door opened, waking me out of my trance. I walked out of the men's room followed closely by the animals yelling at me from North East.

I knew I could not go near that lecturer again, and dropped out of mathematics soon after.

Eating my lunch alone with my thoughts was slowly interrupted by the chewing of another mouth on its own lunch opposite me. This very dark-olive-skinned young man of European appearance then opened his mouth: 'Those two girls are hot bro'—he was a stereotypical Aussie Maronite.

'Then let's talk to them', I responded. It was the logical step.

'Hey Diana and Jackie, how are you? This is my friend, Samuel.'

I left them to it.

The next day, I had my hair out whilst strolling with a tight, blue shirt and baggy jeans when someone jumped on my back. I instantly grabbed them, shifted my body weight and threw them at the ground.

It was Samuel.

'How are ya man,' he yelled with excitement.

With suspicion, I had now memorised his accent and replied back, *'What's up, bro,'* I'm sure he was seeing through the act. 'Let's go out this Saturday night,' he asked me with excitement.

'Tall, dark, and handsome' was the trinity I kept hearing of, so lying in the sun was quickly tried before buying the tanning lotion. So excited at the prospect, I put half the bottle on my face and went to sleep.

The next day, girls were looking at me. All my problems were solved simply by being dark skinned, and I didn't even have to colour my arms.

Isaac, a student, turned around and asked me quietly, 'What happened to you?'

'Why?'

'Man, you look like that,' he said pointing to the orange manila folder on my desk.

So that's why I was being stared at.

'Have you been to the beach lately?,' asked another student.

I heard Isaac laughing in the background.

One thing I gained out of the brief days at uni, besides the increase in knowledge of people, was 'fully sick' Samuel. To this day, I cannot believe that such a character has a PhD in orthoptics.

Having failed my mother again, my depression was sending me into hibernation.

She thought I had natural sales ability which brought me to a job interview about promoting orange juice. 'Do your best,' the manager said. 'You look like you will be popular with the female shoppers.' The best anyone else had done was fifteen bottles over a four-hour period.

The Jamiel that was a face to people around him hid the scared boy who resided within; with his ability to learn how to mimic body language increasing with each passing second as the boy within memorised passing shoppers without a break. The juice aisle belonged to the man controlled by the boy and would be his best performance since playing the piano to 3,000 people when he was 16. It was time to watch this fabricated adult in action when a well-dressed old lady approaching made eye contact with him. I mimicked the eye contact by looking through her, which I had noticed that others didn't notice. Out came in a sly English accent which almost sounded like she was purring, 'I'm going to buy one from you because you're a fox.' It was time to quickly select a reply:

'Well, why don't you buy two?' Within half an hour, I had matched the fifteen-bottle record.

Soon after, I was running to storage to get more.

After three hours, stage Jamiel sold seventy-two bottles and the supermarket was out of stock.

Still paid the full amount, I swung by two whistles and one girl calling out. 'Too good looking to be Lebanese' would be another famous insult to the boy within.

I had to test my DNA someday.

'Were they this superficial?' I was astounded as I hid inside this tanned man with broad shoulders and a short pony tail.

'Were they this superficial,' I now repeated with a grin.

One hour with people to still sell more than the average seller would achieve in four hours for the same pay decreased exposure to the excruciating pain of being outside my room, kept Mum and Dad at bay, showered me with some money, and taught me more about human behaviour.

Now with a girlfriend, I despised her friends who accused me of dishonesty for reasons they refused to explain. Thankfully, one of her friends did not believe the garbage and after being dumped by my first girlfriend after a few weeks, I was invited by this friend to talk with the hope of understanding what I had done to get this outcome. We ended up dating, but she kept sex for her older boyfriend for the few weeks before me walking away when finding out that she was a shoplifter.

FATHER SAM SIMON

They had lied when they said that Father Sam would be fine and when I heard the news, I felt nothing, having witnessed him receding into my memories and staying with me always long ago.

The funeral service was muffled by the church walls as I lay within the small caves that entangled trees had created for me as a child. From here I could be close to the Father whilst away from the hypocrisy of dancing, shouting, and confessions before a piece of wood by those who would then go forth to reoffend.

I was 19 when Father Simon never returned and as life would have it, my faith went with him. It was with dangerous ease that stage Jamiel offered gum to the Italian Liliana. She smiled back at the face that imitated the eye contact of others. Why it was important to Father Simon that I be a millionaire remained elusive to me, but with the powers growing as stage Jamiel absorbed the meaning of more facial expressions, I knew I had to find out.

The distance in time between the crowd and me alone at the graveside was not far. No longer did the person exist whose body was rotting beneath the freshly covered ground with no headstone, and it was now up to me; becoming a millionaire would keep him alive for me. It had to come true.

2002

Almost two years had now past and without boring you with the full story, I had become a locally successful DJ, honing my skills with constantly mixing multiple tracks as though I was mixing colours on canvas, creating something that no one had ever heard and would not hear again.

The desire to always mix live had finally landed me a gig before a full capacity crowd, including the very collected Nathaniel with his magazine-worthy girlfriend, holding up an atmosphere that was almost bursting through the ceiling. It was an experience I never wanted gone, and when two guys who didn't recognise me as the kid they bullied at North East came up to shake my hand, I knew I was hooked.

New Year's Eve 2001 saw a ninety-kilogram man I sometimes felt was me, being approached by Sydney Casino's confident entertainment coordinator. A tall man in his early fifties with a brisk walking pace came straight up to me as soon as I had finished the private gig I was invited to host at the casino. 'We want to open a club on level two and you are the guy.' Overlooking the sea of gamers on poker machines below, he had one request: 'Whatever you do, make sure you do not upset the patrons below,' he warned me. 'Regardless of how well you do here, they pay the casino's bills.' I guessed he was telling me not to play too loudly.

The club snowballed into a greater event with each passing week. Each day I was not Djing was defined by how many days remained until the next event.

Good Friday 2002 was hindsight's climax. Temporarily jumping into families' lives as a mobile DJ was no longer required; the street had jumped into mine. No other club was open and the line to the entrance of my club extended further than I could see. Never had so many people been so disturbingly close as the guards pushed the crowd away from my turntables. People were desperate for a word with the man I had created; the boy within knew that with him exposed, life would have told a different story. One night, soon after the dream I would miss for years to come, a well-known jockey was bashed for not allowing some men to dance with his model girlfriend. Making the papers the next day, the casino abandoned all new projects.

In a desperate attempt to hold on to what was saving my life, I decided to electrically morph lyrics of iconic rappers and singers over Middle Eastern beats. After weeks of adding and removing frequencies for each second of the mutated track, the finished version was broadcast over the airwaves of the western half of Sydney.

The new sound shredded through the city as my phone ceased not to ring with need for a copy of this alien sound.

It was time to combine my baby with this need into a virus that would even be heard coming from cars passing me by. Shocked to turn on the TV to hear my creation played during a halftime show at Sydney's biggest stadium to a full capacity crowd of rugby fans, the older me is needed to articulate the sheer horror of witnessing the ultimate dream of uncountable friends being stolen by those who must have had plenty. The rage he felt was then directed within.

The next two years involved intense study of the Arabic versions of both the New Testament and the Koran, observing Samuel's putrid Saturday night lifestyle filled with anything you can imagine seeing in Sydney's red light district, and becoming absorbed into a crowd of Muslim youth and the subsequent extremist Islamic world that was invisible to even my own family.

Continuing the mimicking of behaviours of others as well as the weight training, the exterior which continued to insulate young Jamiel had become a 188 centimetres, 102 kilograms, shaved head, fake tattoo donning, tanning lotion wearing monster of a human being. Surrounded by families teaching their 5-year-old children to hate Jews never sat right with me, but the doctrine of 'eye for an eye' was a stark deviation from 'turn the other cheek' only showing a younger self the absurdity of all three Abrahamic doctrines without editing.

Assuming the need for violence had left me years before, the young boy in control of the chilling exterior still had one unknown weakness: bullies. Like a dormant volcano which becomes only a mountain in the minds of those living near it, the child would soon become aware of the weakness when spotting an adult bully picking on others as he drove dangerously down the highway.

Never forgetting the lack of power that police possessed, he felt it was up to him to save the innocents from this temporary evil. Calmly, he got out of his car when the bully had stopped his van at the next set of lights while still abusing an innocent passenger, then launching his right leg into the van's passenger door, destroying it as he ripped it open.

Leaning over the passenger seat and lifting the bully out of seat by his chest, I was absolutely shocked to hear the obvious lie whimpered forth as though a dog's tail had been stepped upon: 'I'm innocent! I haven't done anything!'

With the knowledge of my weakness, no promise against violence could be complete without the impressive person keeping me safe, being held accountable. I forced the heavy man back into his car, and despite having to DJ a gig that day, I took him straight to the police station where I was held for two hours, waiting for the man in the van to report the incident.

The last gig

With one last attempt at friends, months were spent preparing what would be the second and final event ever self-produced. It wasn't long before the night was assaulted by hurling eggs, the breaking down of the main doors, and a fire set to the building. Having nothing left to live for apart from the seven guys that followed me home, I decided that I would spend the last of what I owned on losing my virginity and would take these young men with me.

Made known to me by Samuel, an unlit factory appeared in the grey lighting from the outside, which was instantly forgotten once the heavy set doors were pushed open; the red-carpeted stairs, high ceilings, and solid furnishings of the interior were of a palace hidden within a dump.

An attractive blonde showed the young boys into the waiting room, where our game of pool was interrupted by little MG's gaze upon a woman with legs that looked as though they could run the Melbourne cup.

We handed him over.

Like a mother dragging a child out of a shop, MG disappeared from view whilst encouraged by our thumbs up.

A little lacking in class, the next lady caught Ahmed's eye whilst yelling at us to shut up; before more gracious ladies grabbed the rest.

Not wanting this as a first experience was what I used as a guide to actually proceed with this loveless act; considering any natural instincts of mine had done nothing but produce the life witnessed upon earlier pages. Sonya was Italian, 39, had a boyfriend, and refused to believe I was a virgin. Still resisting her advances, we spoke for most of the time until she visited upon me pressure to move on with the act as time was running out.

After so many years of waiting, it was the chase for desert water to only spit out sand. 'Spending time with myself was better' was the major thought on my mind's merry-go-round whilst showering in a futile attempt to rid the feeling of disgust so entrenched in so little time.

When MG reappeared, his friends' reactions told me he'd had the best birthday and Christmas presents all rolled into one. He decided to rename himself from 'the black dude' to 'the man-whore'.

It was time to break away from an ideology that was now resulting in attacks upon infidel neighbours. Breaking my cover, I openly criticised them for attacking people who had done them no wrong, and that perhaps they feared their own homosexual impulses or perhaps the success of the 'infidels' against the failure to integrate into such a contrasting society by their parents. I did see Ahmed many years later working as a security guard in the same shopping mall that took my teeth as Ahmed was just becoming a teenager. Goodness trapped within an ideology, I missed his friendship for years to come.

January 2004

. . .saw me standing at the airport, waiting for Mum and Dad to return from their second honeymoon. It was the shuttle bus that caught my eye, and after memorising the location of the 300 hotels in the CBD with the aid of twenty-four hours and little big brother Micah, my van was a door-to-door service. The first day was as though the era of old, when Micah and I were a born team with only second nature between us. By the second day, he was gone and I spent the day looking for hotel doors.

Missing the door in a one-way street during rush hour would delay my trips by hours until a backpacker exiting the bus told me: *'You know you don't have to go to every hotel door'*. My reply was logical: *'But then it wouldn't be a door-to-door service?'*

He explained that it was not lying to stop between two hotels, but I had no limit on how far apart these hotels could be from each other. Escorting passengers off the bus and pointing to their hotel six blocks away allowed this job to grab me dollars like points in computer games I had grown up with. Now working over 100 hours a week, it was time to upgrade my licence. More points came with more passengers, and repeating the memorised phrases over hundreds of hours had them fluent enough to keep my past life hidden. The game was becoming boring and without the desire for wealth for its own sake, it was time for the only partially awkward man in his mid-twenties to escape to the cool mountains overlooking the shimmering city of the Levant's pearl, this time to become a translator.

BECOMING A TRANSLATOR
July 2004
Jounieh, Eastern Mediterranean

Without street signs, I scanned the terrain whilst super positioning pictures from my mind until I knew to which building to carry these two large bags in the thirty-five degree heat.

Ninety minutes later and after a cold shower, it was time to hear the laughter bursting forth from family members upon hearing my plans followed by anger that I was boarding at the university campus. Left again not understanding the emotions misread, I settled into the private university full of children of the well-heeled. Snuggled into the top of a mountain overlooking magnificent expanses of green valley which disappeared into the Mediterranean by day, and the lights of the robust life by night, the advanced course in Arabic I was promised over the phone was apparently not in existence by the time I had arrived. Furious at being lied to and having no idea why, I stood quietly on the balcony of my student apartment; staring at the vast expanse of the blue sea, broken only by the now infamous golden shimmer of a retreating sun as it crossed Europe and over to the Americas. The nothingness of a closed student apartment left no defence against the deafening videos roaring past the back of my eyes like a high-speed train; embarrassment of past lives described in pages prior, mixed with the realisation that behind the act lay the same, stupid fool who understood—and was understood by no one. Depression had evolved these days into black ice crawling through my bones, and through gaps between the screams from ancient memories still strong, I stood at the balcony's edge, dreaming of falling off.

The one thing that hadn't changed was the mountain overlooking Dad's birthplace, by then convinced that time must have been relative only to the apparent decay of an object and that there must have been layers of perceived timelines, with the one we all lived in seeming less real with each gaze at the monster being passed by the sun.

The retired village professor attributed my capabilities to my Arabic-speaking background, which I felt conflicted with the fact that I didn't have one—but I could see a shadow of Father Simon in this man: patient, respectful, and sometimes lunching together at his home with his wife. Like most Maronites, his children had immigrated to first world countries to lead lives of quiet success as what most people would stereotypically perceive to be 'Italians' or 'Greeks.' Like the Irish, most Maronites lived outside their tiny homeland to never return, leaving the old professor to view his dying world for his remaining days as more and more Arab refugees poured over the barren Anti-Lebanon mountains that once protected his Mediterranean homeland from the Middle East.

It was time for the American and European ex-pats to spend their summer at bikini-clad beach parties both more Western than, and isolated from, the Western world itself, with the younger ones staying out late in the cool, mountain air. It was my chance to relive a youth more successful than the first time around, and now being judged as 'cool,' I had helped ease some of my real past's traumatic memories.

It was time to buy a tent and enjoy sleeping directly against the mountainous backdrop, and on the way to buy a tent, a blindingly white BMW in the blazing sun caught my eye. Using a large number of the points built up back in Australia, I blew my budget on desiring freedom to head into the mountains as I did those years before with the red-headed delivery driver. The reaction was unexpected, with Eugene appearing from nowhere to be my friend whilst being invited to two weddings. It became clear that people were interested in money, and I hated them for it.

It was time to rent a smaller car and just drive—driving to borders between regions, religions, countries, towns, and even languages. It was hitchhiking in fast forward but with social study by observation without interaction.

Hours of self-reflection whilst stopping only for fuel brought back an unusual memory from six years before, where Uncle Randy had told me a story about his past with one very different key detail when hearing the same story but from Uncle 'Pretty Boy' Henry during one of my stops at his place.

'There is no conclusion possible other than that Uncle Randy lied'—this bothered me as I recalled both videos side by side and over and over, watching how Uncle Randy had crossed his legs away from me and his wife when making the statement, how he said it in a voice that was inconsistent with his usual tone, how it was so important to make such a benign comment about a relationship with another woman prior to his late marriage.

'Why would he lie . . . but even worse . . . how he could live this long without admitting that he did lie in front of his supposedly beloved grandnephew, his wife, and children?'

There was no way of shaking this feeling which I had to share with the wife of my dad's brother I haven't yet mentioned, an older brother named after John the Baptist whom one could easily confuse with my own father. No other family member would be tolerant of such observations about their beloved uncle, and I was very fortunate to have possibly given birth to the idea that he may not have needed to be so beloved.

Never would my father travel away without Mum, and his surprise journey here saw him sleeping on a swinging bed, whilst I spent my breakfasts at the empty snack bar next to my grandfather's grave, keeping the company of the broad-shouldered mountain as it gazed into the perfect blue skies, day after day.

Gazing at the densely filled, starry nights, I would oscillate between times past—losing vast expanses of time in the present. It was during one of the brief moments back under the stars that I heard sounds of distress being carried down to Grandad's grave from above. It was Uncle John's wife with whom I left the idea about Uncle Randy's true character, exchanging controlled but heated words with Uncle Randy's evil son Eugene. How this bright woman had finally seen through the manipulative Eugene was almost a miracle, but that no one had seen it since we were kids was a concept unprocessable by my faulty brain. Eugene was calmly playing chess against three silly brothers, with their love for his father not letting them see that Eugene was only his father's pawn; being used to distract them whilst he stole millions of dollars intended to be inherited by my father from his dead father, whom I discovered from future research was a symbol of hatred by his baby brother Randy for reasons I can only partially ascertain.

I grabbed my father's jaw, a shadow of how I remembered it as a child, and calmly whispered: *'Don't you see, Dad, this is what he wants.'*

Dad was furious and listened to nothing I was saying. His elder clone of a brother, John, then let out his rage:

'you came here just to turn me against my own uncle?'

Uncle Pretty Boy was shocked to see his nephew more in control than he, asking his baby brother to listen to his son. Delaying the inevitable by at least ten minutes, I knew that these three were no match for a psychopath who had already planned for his son to record their heated conversation to use against them in court if they would ever dare get the courage to pursue their elder. Turning his cousins against their uncle, Eugene had successfully become next in line for the millions stolen by his father. Not knowing what I was by any stretch at that age, I still knew that only one person could damage their plan. I would have to strike back that evening.

The autistic vs the psychopath

I smiled at Uncle Randy as I popped my head through the curtain, separating his outdoor setting from his front yard. I had come to thank his son for being so straightforward about how he felt about his uncles, and how it was great to have someone to talk to who saw my father's generation as inexperienced.

I could learn from him as his son clearly did, about how ignorant my father's brothers were and that he was wrong to love them over his son—as he had stated to me numerous times at my parents place back in Sydney.

My calm manner seemed to infuriate him against his own son who was losing his temper, with the prize finally awarded to me when he asked me if *'you came here just to turn me against my own son?'*

Wow. Perhaps Eugene had taught me something after all.

I simply explained that *'I am here just to confirm the truth that you both know, and with the best of intentions—just as Eugene did just a few hours ago.'*

Uncle Randy was too angry to continue chatting, which left me the opportunity to say to the psychopath: *'I know you think you are the smartest guy here, but just remember that I did to you what you did to less intelligent people this evening. I think that makes me smarter, don't you think?'*

He scrunched up his face as though there was a bad smell which I could not detect. Not understanding what this meant, I returned home to Uncle John's wife giving me a gigantic hug after hearing the story.

Not realising it then, it makes the most sense to think that a small idea planted in the mind of the woman I describe as 'Uncle John's best decision' was what allowed her to anticipate the evil that lived not far from her which has, over the years, resulted in numerous lawsuits against the now old and miserable Uncle Randy who would barely traverse his home town in public again.

All the 23-year-old knew was that it was time to leave his girlfriend whom he was not aware was also a sex worker, to head back with Dad to his real home.

Dad departed first, which left me sitting in corners of night clubs to continue observing the phenomenon of 'dancing', but before long I would, too, see Cyprus, the liquid gold of the setting sun across the waves, and the desert of Syria as the green and white mountains of Dad's old home faded with the sea. It was beautiful.

(The day the pope came)

1986

> *Mum dropped me off that warm, sunny day. I loved that no student had yet arrived, leaving me waiting for life to appear whilst I sat at one of the many wooden benches, looking out at the field and its timber forts.*
>
> Reliving this memory, I had to get my 5-year-old version to speak to the maintenance man, to ask him where all the people were.
>
> *I had been sitting there for almost three hours before the man advised that the pope was in town and that no one was coming to school today. He got a parent for me, who provided me a yummy lunch at her home alongside her frizzy haired, 11-year-old daughter whilst calling home until the early afternoon when Mum would answer.*

It's hard to start at 23 was the recurring theme. *'It would not be until 31 that any potential friendship had reached even 8 years'*—was the repeated voice of anxiety, as videos of those who rightly labelled me as the loser were set on auto loop whilst my fellow Australians moved on with their lives. Pain would bring pain, but joy would be worse, as it would bring back the above thoughts that were always the prequel to new anxiety. The fear of the anxiety was now worse than the anxiety itself.

Licence after licence, creating the DJ school bus that became so popular after Micah helped me wire my old discman into the Bus P.A. system, driving coaches and meeting older and more affluent couples, then getting into the big rigs. It was my first ever proper girlfriend with such gorgeous, African skin who explained that I would never find anyone better than her. I agreed with her throughout the eight-month relationship, considering she was still popular amongst her school colleagues despite having finished high school not long after I had, by now being about 6 whole years. She did help cover my explosions of syllables from her friends, and ordered me not to ask questions to them that came naturally to me such as *'What do you think about the situation in post-communist Eastern Europe?'* or *'What is your position on consciousness and the human brain?'*

Her friends acted very much like the bullies of old and being around them was frightening, but my love's swearing at me to get over it was enough to force me back into what could only make me stronger.

I can thank my first love for two things, with the first being the below:

On a fourteen-day cruise where I would spend my time walking around the ship, memorising any patterns that stood out, a rotating wheel caught my eye. It was surrounded by only a few fascinated people, a table of numbers, and a quiet woman in a suit, spinning a tiny ball around its insides.

The suited woman kindly explained the rules of the game, and then it all made sense.

The numbers told me a story, and with each spin of the wheel, the story continued. With each new number, I innately knew what group of numbers would be on its way. The quiet woman continued explaining more of the game's details, whilst my giggling friends continued to whisper what no one else seemed to hear. They made me feel special as time brought us closer. Why was no one else betting on the correct sequence? Never did my new friends make fun of me, and so it was time to place some money down.

I used this toy to pay for my lunch each day.

ADRIENNE
11ᵗʰ of January 2014

It took ten months to know that I would never see what Jamiel does.

I finally persuaded him to get back to the casino.

Why wouldn't he lay eggs if they were golden?

He knew where every machine was but there was no showing off;

he just knew where to go, and went.

I couldn't tell if he was calculating or simply nervous, but he knew which group of numbers would be next every time. How? And why would he not bet?

As quiet as always, I enjoyed his presence as crowds fluttered back and forth, losing their chips whilst he whispered how much each person was losing.

Before he amassed enough data, they changed the guy at the table.

He said it didn't really matter, but it would just take a little longer.

The dealer kept his gaze on him when he could be free of the wandering fools.

It was that he kept reminding me of his chances of 'not losing' with each spin.

After being satisfied with his chip building, he smiled like a child and said, 'Let's go to the big boy table.'

I had to know what calculations were in his head that would lead him to bet on a number.

Was he reckless, or the calculating genius I believed he was?

200 per cent return was enough for him.

He took the cash and we had some Chinese.

He got me a nice drink. He always gets nice drinks.

I decided he wasn't reckless at all, with opportunities taken only when odds were well in his favour.

Adrienne

A night away from my room, and well into the thick haze of depression, I was in a hotel room while my gorgeous, African girlfriend was asleep. I was desperately trying to silence the screams within my head by banging my head against the hotel wall. The pain kept me from facing the internal screaming alone. My first love kept on in sleep with no idea of my cries for death.

I needed out of this body, out of this life.

Unforeseen, Mum one day cleared her schedule whilst having me sit before a young doctor who asked rhetorical questions, such as, 'On the scale of one to ten, how strong is your urge to kill yourself?'

My answer had me awarded two lollies with the strange name of Valium followed by a lift home by Mum for a quick nap.

Thirty-six hours had passed and I could smell the goodness emanating from the kitchen where Dad would spend hours each day, but as though I just dropped a sack of potatoes I had been carrying for twenty-four years, there was something missing. I could see around me only the present; the thoughts were gone. Like a blind man seeing for the first time, I could not explain what this new state of consciousness was apart from that the past was now far away and I was fine; nothing but fine. Two pills, once off, and all those years of hell had disappeared.

The second awarding of thanks to my first love was for her looking for a new job, finding one which looked great but that she wasn't so sure about for some bizarre reason. Hoping to convince her, I posted forth another movie line: *'If you don't apply for this, then I will.'*

Unfortunately, this plan backfired as I then had to apply for the job. Two weeks later, I was faced with two job offers and asked trusty brother Micah, *'Should I take this commission based sales job, or the full-time interstate trucking one?'*

We sat in Mum and Dad's new house overlooking the water, before a view that couldn't care which way the decision went. Knowing my young self until now, I am sure you may have guessed which path he would take.

I was accepted into the one-week-long training session, where the confident and charismatic Englishman displayed his talent for me to observe.

'I am going to teach you how to sell a mortgage, and out of every 200 people that come here, less than 10 survive.'

'I don't even know what a mortgage is,' I thought to myself.

Spending the week with his behaviour allowed me to memorise his walk, the way he leaned his body depending upon the words being used, how long he spent making eye contact with each person in the room, his voice levels, the accents he placed on each word, and much more than I care to list. It was now my turn to present to both him and his right hand man, Mr Chowdry.

Mimicking the memories of him, I followed the video with pure fluency to its end, hiding behind my suited body in preparation for the feedback. For less than a second, I noticed a flash of silence greater than what had been after any other student's mock presentation thus far. It was only then that the small audience broke out into an applause not heard for any other candidate for the sales role.

Supposedly, I reminded him of himself when he first started.

Although commanded to use the company's pre-recorded figures as examples of client savings, I could see the blink rate of the eyes of my potential new clients slow right down when these numbers were presented to them. The connection was made that perhaps my new-found friends needed the presenting of their own numbers; how would a new mortgage affect them?

That's when I became conscious of knowing the client-desired results as soon as they wrote their numbers down before me. Showing those who had no apparent knowledge of their own finances what power they could have gave me an intrinsic joy and self-worth as of yet undiscovered. Garbage spewing 'sales-people' were repulsive to me, and becoming one of them was not going to happen.

Looking back, I can remember countless people being very silent as they would see me write down their savings as though the first half of their own story fluently memorised by me beforehand. I assumed most people could do this, and always wondered why they would need some young kid to explain the obvious. Desperation deepened with the prescribed drugs becoming increasingly important; their side effects joining me in the abyss of torture. My increasing client base didn't mind, and so I helped them between sleeping and defending against wanting to die.

The final suicide

It was evening beyond evening of decay into ultimate desolation and depression, and after a lifetime of waiting came the night I could finally let go of the guilt of both leaving the family to move on and of the guilt of the God which would punish me for wanting only to end this torture so gifted by him in the very first place.

Letting go was better than the final day of school, and not knowing what was to come I ascended the next bus heading north, perfectly away from all sources of pain I had known. My phone rang. It was my dad and not wanting him the head-start to my intentions, I answered.

'Wherr arr U? U coming hom?'

If only I could ever speak an untruth, I could have explained I was on my way home.

'I'm saying goodbye.'

I hung up.

Mum called from down the coast.

'You worried your father. Where are you?'

I couldn't tell her

She pleaded with me.

I hung up but she kept calling; something she had never done. The intense attention received through the ringing of the phone was like witnessing the holy grail, until the guilt of not answering grew too strong.

I heard a weeping woman through the phone frantically sending forth her undying love. Her horror at the thought of losing this tortured being who, for the first time in living memory seemed a part of her, brought forth a new level of self-disgust, and I wanted to hate her for pulling me back from hell's border with freedom. Why would one need another to continue suffering for the simple reason of the knowledge of their existence? If I didn't meet Dad, I was sure this frantic woman would have the state looking for me before the night's end. There had to be a way to leap over the edge without their knowing.

I rang Dad back and told him I'd meet him at the bus junction. He was waiting.

'Prromise you not do any-sing sdupid.'

Leaving this body wasn't stupid.

'I won't.'

Heading upstairs and straight to the bathroom, locking the door behind me, I called my first love to hear the tenderest goodbye she had ever given.

It was time to leave.

Filling the bath with water, I swallowed every drug I had ever been prescribed and waited for by breathing to slow down. Not more than twelve seconds later, I slowly unpacked my pocket knife, placing the blunt tip against my left wrist. As reality began to feel more like a dream, I dug deep, feeling no pain whilst watching the dark blood begin its march out of and down my wrist before I began slashing even deeper.

Each stab in my wrist was a relief from the room in which I had been entrapped for so many years. My true companion all these years, pain was always there to greet me and it was its turn to say goodbye.

The dark, rich blood was fascinating to watch. I was excited of what was to come, if anything at all. I was becoming sleepy. The knife was not sharp enough, and so I stabbed harder to get between the bones in my way. I am sure I could hear my Father calling for me from somewhere in the house, partially disguised by the blasting forth of water behind me. The combination sounded like a tribal drum from beneath a waterfall.

It was ecstasy.

Before I could fall into the bath, Dad called out through the door, 'Let me in.' He thumped and hammered against it, while I stabbed and sliced with decreasing strength. The short but very solid man eventually found the strength to break down the door to witness his son and his blood-covered arm, with the last thing I remember being him grabbing the much larger human being away from the scene.

I have a flash of being carried down the stairs whilst being surrounded by yelling, followed by darkness.

PART 3

Hoping to be now deceased, I was encouraged by the blinding white light in every direction. Like the parting of the Red Sea, the light began gathering in certain locations, until it converged into the sun streaming in through the glass doors at the end of the hallway. The other end of the hall way expanded out into what looked like a very large room with doctors and nurses walking back and forth. Focusing in on what was immediately before me, I could see a bandaged arm over a blanket. I was under the blanket and the bandaged arm was mine. Smells of fresh bed sheets was a good sign, but the chemical smells of a hospital were not. Fear and Anxiety were rushing towards me from outside the hospital. They knew I was alive and were coming for me once again. Hoping I was dead with one last effort, I now noticed my Mum sitting to my right. I was alive.

The doctors had wondered with Mum how I had survived without any apparent brain damage. I was wondering how Mum had been able to arrive back to Sydney so quickly, until it was explained to me that more than two days had passed since me being brought here. Mum had not left the bedside since she had arrived.

Mum

With Mum apparently instigating a conversation, it was surprisingly awkward. Mum was a fatalist, it seems; as she coolly explained that it was not yet my time to leave—with too many people's lives I was changing for the better that still needed changing, and that I was truly different from others. You may expect to take compliments from your mother with less gravity for reasons an older self would discover as he met more mothers in other families, but you also may now have an idea of my mum's 'matter of fact' character and thereby see why a detached boy just out of a coma would take that comment so seriously. Perhaps I wasn't slower than most, but rather faster than all—the born again atheist over adjusting to now live only for others, and thereby understanding Father Simon's prophecy in a new way: destiny would have my suffering dwarfed by the brilliance shining from a foreign source within me upon others.

The incomplete journey to death is one that will inevitably be finalised, with me now living in what seemed a state of limbo. Detached from the life unfolding before me, as though from behind thick glass, I watched the young adult continue on the path that perhaps had to continue for now.

It was time to discover his powers, and how he could defend others from the evils of the world in which we were all stuck.

The Next Chapter

Accidentally finding out that I was bringing in 40 per cent of the company's new business against the sixteen others, my contempt for these self-loving, materialistic, egos which saw their clients as dollar signs was made worse by them making fun of me for being the first at the food table after their stupid weekly meetings which I was, for some unexplained reason, forced to attend.

With each knock at a new door was a new family and new phrases learned. The psychiatrist that Mum and I were now visiting was the first to ever explain the emotional meaning of the *'Hello, how are you'* exchange. It was the first time the connection between words and emotional meaning delivered by words was ever made for me, and I quickly began looking for patterns between words and why they were used, like discovering a new dimension on a number plane that was always there. I had now deduced that the response of 'good' was almost always a lie when combined with the conversations I could hear from family members in different rooms. Each member had an issue I would absorb while listening to my hosts divulging their financial circumstances. The next shock was learning that no matter how nice my hosts were, they would end up lying at least once during the evening. Why would they openly lie to me when the contradiction was so easily verifiable by the numbers on bank statements that they themselves would present me with? I had to create a hypothesis: if there truly was this emotional dimension that I could not see, then there could also be a barrier between people that could only be crossed through establishing an emotional connection. I mentioned this to the doctor who explained this as *'breaking the ice'*; so like a surfer riding a wave, words must have conveyed meanings for normal people that were carried by the words themselves.

My brain sent forth a new thought: that perhaps these people didn't remember the words uttered at all, but some sort of emotional meaning they felt when the words were received by them.

Irrespective, if there was any chance of me helping any human, I would have to learn their language. There was still the hardened housewife that no one at work wanted to help as no commission was involved; there was no way I was leaving her case alone.

As the prescribed drugs slowed me back down into the world of the images in my head, I began to hear my own voice. Memories were shades of what they were, but time was now linear. The slow process of each past event realigning into its distance from the present was physically painful, and the strength to end this life was slowly returning. Able to focus, sitting down with others, listening to others tell me things I truly had no interest in, maintaining eye contact, and holding down a job. The normal world was condoning the success I didn't value, and condoned the new me discovered through medication.

'Why do you want to help this woman so much, Jamiel? There isn't much commission in it for the amount of visits you are making there.' I didn't like the smirk branded across Chowdry's bony face; it was inconsistent with the genuineness of the question. It was my fault for somehow not explaining myself correctly—all the more reason to get this tough woman back the strength she and her boys deserved. By now I had an idea, but it would have to wait.

After three months of giving up on relationships, Mum decided it was time to get involved.

Since last seeing her as a child, Sabrina had become a global force in her own right, heading a multinational, multi-billion-dollar firm. Throughout this majestic transition, the now grown woman had remained a loyal client of Mum's, allowing me to trust Mother's judgement of Sabrina's exemplary character.

Allowing the grown man to fluently align responses from the ever-growing bank of phrases, I focused on regulating my tone and speed of speech whilst on the phone with Sabrina.

Embarrassed at initially avoiding my call under the assumption that I was someone else, Sabrina suggested we go out for coffee. It bugged me that she would pretend not to hear a person, even if it was to avoid someone not deserving of a conversation, but how could I say no?

ME: "So your Mum set you up on a date with Aunty Sabrina? THE Aunty Sabrina? My Aunty Sabrina? Hahahaha!"
Jamiel: "Why is that so funny, Adrienne?"
ME: "Because she's my Aunt, and you're Jamie"
Jamiel: "And the sky is a combination of the sun and our atmosphere. What that has to do with anything reminds me of how strange you regular humans are to me"
ME: "Ok, Jamiel. Back to the story, chop chop."
Jamiel: "But you are the one who interrupted the story?!"
ME: "Can you please just continue, Jamiel."
He was frustrated now, Even his generally stoic face couldn't hide that.
I knew I would have to ask Aunty Sabrina to tell me her version of meeting Jamiel after I heard Jamie's. I would end up getting that story many months later, but I'll tell it to you before I share with you the version told to me by the now frustrated Jamiel.

Letters from Sabrina
Part one—Re-meeting Jamiel

If anybody had ever asked whether 'I remembered Jamiel?' I would have replied, 'that irritating kid that wouldn't shut up.' When he appeared at the door, I saw the kid.

Within the first glance, the kid was replaced with a tall, strong jaw-lined pretty face, thick brown hair, blond eyebrows, almond eyes that shone like emeralds set in gold, and the most dazzling smile—and I remember taking a breath.

That day, he was controlled; proud of his steep gain in income after learning about what a mortgage was. He also noticed that I was unimpressed. The waitress handed me his strawberry milkshake, which we laughed about whilst I realised that I would be missing my favourite TV show. Hilariously, Jamiel kept a pocket TV with him which saved the day as we sat in his tiny smart car. His car did look ridiculously small for him. I froze when he tenderly asked me if I minded his hand caressing my neck. He was sweet when my answer caused him to pull his hand away and stay next to me while we admired the view of the bay and the airport runway.

Before time could shine upon me more of who this man was, Jamie seemed simply a regular guy who was mathematically gifted; having him refinance my mortgage after being dazed with incredulity by his streaming forth of mortgage projections with neither pen nor paper, only to confirm his calculations with a spreadsheet I kept secret. This view evolved before I could take notice when I took him with me to meet my friends. I asked him whether he would come with me to 'Myer's', and it occurred to me only at the front door of my friend 'Mya's' place that he had thought I was referring to the department store. He was scared to enter a strange home, but assured me he would be fine to go inside when I suggested we not enter.

At first, he was well liked, and his cheeks would redden with bashful excitement. I thought he was trying to impress when he would remember a crowd of names upon hearing them all in succession for the first time, and even though he certainly succeeded, I soon discovered he had no idea why they were so fascinated.

Nonetheless, what crept in to the light was that he would tend to sit away from others. His conversations led away from the flow of the group, with his interest in anyone on a personal level in short supply. When people asked him how his week was, he would literally discuss the condition of his past week with facts galore, leaving those around him feeling stupid. He kept coming across as arrogant, but when alone, he was so sweet.

The weeks progressed, and my love for him grew, and he mentioned in passing about his seeing of counsellors. Our tale was stripped of fairies soon after, when a very funny story about a green-eyed classmate in high school caused Jamie to freeze, and then retreat into oblivion for ten minutes. Before me was only a beautiful mannequin, and when he returned it was someone else. Unresponsive, he began to hyperventilate before lying down.

Struck with sheer terror, I shivered whilst hearing the words
'I don't want you to see this.'

A cold breeze rushed down my throat and into my back. Some girl and some formal from his past were the stabs in his chest that would eventually heal just so it could be stabbed again.

I sat, simply shocked, while he swallowed medication that would carry him into a stone-cold slumber. Like a child, I had him blanketed, then shivered in fear of this terrible secret I would have to keep from my parents.

I was desperate to know of the oblivion into which he had fell, but he brought it up not once. It was days later that I could wait no longer, and so I took him through what I went through during the traumatic episode I had to witness that week. He apparently didn't remember the episode. I was seeing him every day, witnessing his nightmares, and using them as a portal to the past in a way I could only dream of ever remembering things. His blinding capacity was clearly both unnoticed and as of yet unmeasured, as much as it saddened me to know its curse that had plagued him since birth. I was furious at a God that would allow such sweetness to suffer so much. At times he would be embarrassed when thrown back into the present knowing I'd been there the whole time. According to his words, he lived amongst constant and concurrent videos and flashes through time that would never cease, whilst trying to be with me in 'my' reality. Not knowing any peace, withstanding insanity was a miracle I couldn't comprehend. I cried when he whimpered that being snapped out of it was like having icy water thrown over him every time.

I can still hear the screams when he walked silently into the bedroom and put his face against a pillow.

Pages out of my diary were filled with nonsense in the hope of finding some pattern, some sense to this madness. I lost myself in supporting him; I could feel his pain, and it was killing me.

I had always thought we were born with the ability to stop a conversation, learning that his thoughts were like wild, runaway horses that just had to do what they do. He needed the poisonous Diazepam, and I would let it tear me apart so he could get some sleep. Coming out of the shower, I can't even explain what I went through when I saw him looking out the kitchen window while holding the largest kitchen knife to his chest. With the last shred of my sense of identity, I once turned the car back home to grab his medication and jolt him out of unresponsiveness, only to find when I returned, his seat-belt wrapped tightly around his neck.

Re-meeting Sabrina
(Jamiel's perspective)

When she opened the door, I was surprised at how much shorter than me she had become, although losing none of her beauty, with her gigantic black eyes, olive skin, and chestnut hair. The recent past had taught me a new look that I had learned to pattern to women's faces, and there it was before me once again. Mutual attraction was instant.

She guided me to a beach café, where I ordered my strawberry milkshake to the surprise of both her and the waitress who casually handed it to her. It was a surprise to enjoy a conversation with someone, and her obviously superior social skills kept me enthralled. It was fantastic to have no reaction to the leap in my salary from bus driver to mortgage consultant, although simultaneously embarrassing that she may have mistaken my comment for one who was attempting a boast— as opposed to the Jamiel who was simply stating facts and figures. It was great to have someone like me as much as I did them. She had the power to keep Depression outside when I entered her place, and during her trips overseas I was left to face the walls of her apartment, to hear the sounds of families, of cars, and the trees. Multiple conversations were teaching me more about how to speak as one of them, with the shallow speech like a virus I had to absorb. Talking to Sabrina for hours by phone alleviated the depression and the anxiety, keeping me away from an estranged brother and distant family. I missed the colours and animations of my free mind, and in the willing absence of the drugs, the images flooded back. I became immobilised, swallowing Diazepam, and sometimes driving late night streets. Sometimes I'd run.

Letters from Sabrina
Part two

Days and nights merged for me soon after, hating myself for daring to fall asleep, when he would sleep on the floor after pleading to stay.

It seemed as though Jamie had no one in his corner, where I would only have to scratch myself to have phone calls from family members in an instant.

A man in whom lived a child starved of nurturing, I wanted to be all things to him—but I bordered on controlling. How could I help it? His innocence needed guidance and protection.

He started on video games to tie down his mind, and I would comment despite knowing he would never be guided, ordered, or told. He was a shooting star that was shooting himself in the foot. His anger at me if interrupting his game playing was almost unbearable, but he could swallow any perceived pride in an instant and say *'I want to be here with you.'*

One way to suck him out of his crowded mind was to get him to focus momentarily on a photo and describe it in detail with his eyes closed. I loved witnessing this ability.

I'd get the calculator out and enjoy his minute grin as he picked up the right answer.

The sheer power of his mind was undeniable, and so I continued probing almost blindly for a way for him to push back against its control over him; with the hope that he would one day harness its extraordinary power.

I tried to explain to him that the dishonesty and corruption that was everywhere he looked at work was the real world to everyone else.

A concept to him completely insoluble, I'd let him rant about helping his clients achieve the success they deserved and if that meant he'd have to start his own firm then so be it. Helping others gave him an energy that excited me and those around him, and with him becoming socially aware for the first time in his life, it was time to witness a star rising, but there was still so much for him to learn—like not fronting up to someone's door with sunnies on: 'Jamiel, you scare people; take off the glasses and your jacket and fold it over your arm and smile when someone opens the door.' He found how much difference that made, and added this to his ever-growing list of social gestures.

Jamiel waking up to the dark desires of humans

Could it have been possible that Mr Chowdry wasn't aware that the firm was receiving ongoing commissions over and above the huge fee they were attaching to each mortgage? I certainly was not aware of this.

The English man I had learned to copy was, to me, now a charlatan, but Sabrina wasn't surprised at what she specified was simply the 'world'. This brave new world was rewarding the dumping of newly mortgaged clients to proceed with new sales. Mr Chowdry asked me why I kept visiting clients for whom I had already received my one-off commission. I explained to him that I had discovered that they were not being guided after signing on with the firm, and were (in human speak) "falling off the rails". Was it possible that Mr Chowdry and this firm was only interested in feeding off the flesh of clients, only to leave them to fend for and die by themselves? What sort of company was this? How could Sabrina accept this as the "world"?

I needed a break from this suicide inducing reality. Not sure of what to do, I hopped on a plane—this time to the Far East—where the only person's guidance I could trust was now residing. As Sydney once again disappeared behind me, I was free and heading to what perhaps would have been the end of the earth for my Semitic ancestors.

Sabrina
(In the Far East)

Jamie was a tall and broad-shouldered man with the innocence of a child. He had seen so much, and yet understood so little of what was around him. He was already greeting me in the Shanghainese, Mandarin Dialect language upon his arrival, followed by so many moments of simple joy—from shopping and bargaining, to the special treatment the locals gave us.

It was during one of these little trips that I burst into tears in the supermarket: not even knowing how to order meat in this strange country. Before I could wipe my eyes, I noticed Jamiel hopping and staggering up to locals, making strange gestures accompanied by animal noises. He discovered which meat was which, and then brought them to the cashier while confirming their names in the language I still could not understand.

He left a few days later, speaking enough Mandarin to discuss the weather and traffic with the local taxi drivers. I shouldn't have felt threatened by his emerging capabilities, but I did anyway.

Taking some computers he had bought at a local Chinese factory with him, he then sold them in Sydney with enough of a profit to book a return trip to me.

Jamiel

I returned to work to be faced by Mr Chowdry whilst my suit-donning body went through the process of pouring hot water into a cup of coffee powder. Sabrina had now taught me how to walk in a way that further disguised my mind's peculiarity, whilst I had simultaneously learned to measure day-to-day activities by constantly counting the seconds they would take for others, like making coffee as people seemed to like doing. I asked him about the ongoing commissions and whether the clients were serviced.

Over time, this would prove to be the wrong move, but it was now time to surprise Sabrina with a second visit.

Sabrina
(Back in the Far East)

It wasn't long before he surprised me with a return trip, where he couldn't stop comparing the percentage difference of every McDonald's item to its Sydney-based equivalent on the fly. Night fall dawned whilst we strolled past the families playing in the fairy lit park. He could not contain his joy, dancing like the big child that he was, at the idea of families enjoying a park filled with year-'round Christmas lights at 11.00 p.m.

Back outside my apartment, where the black pond was over lit by white fairies surrounded by a sea of skyscrapers was where he brought out the ring, and although a little too soon, it was picture-perfect.

Jamiel

Getting down on one knee that perfect evening reminded me of how the world must look from Sabrina's head height.

Back in Sydney and with the help of memories of books past, I would bring flowers and gifts, but like with the effects of inflation, each flower was worth a little less than its predecessor and soon became as though I was a child running the wrong way up an escalator . . . trying harder and achieving less; until the day I was asked to activate a light switch located two metres from me but only above her head. Explaining clearly why it made no logical sense to acquiesce to such a bizarre command only helped generate fume from Sabrina's cheeks. Was she crazy, or was I truly missing something? There was no logical explanation that I could see.

The continued pattern of being wrongly judged for unintended behaviour had finally invaded my fiancée's place after suffering severe side effects from medication, vomiting hidden contents from an empty stomach before collapsing onto her living room floor for what turned out to be hours. It was Sabrina's permanent move overseas that her unconscious partner could now not assist her with, but although her anger may be obvious to you, it remained in no way understandable to me, and for those very reasons, I will dive through the icy water where the past me still hides, and let him tell you this story:

2007

We don't have much time before Future Jamiel has to leave, so I will be quick.

I sat on the floor before Sabrina
Looking up at her hurt face
The grey light from the overcast day behind me
I was looking for the energy I needed to be as angry as I was, confused as I was
'How are you mad when I am the one suffering?'
She sat before me and said nothing
As though perhaps I should have
Or that she was tired of being with someone who didn't serve her.
I needed her to understand the grave sin she was committing.
I was not a dog to submit to every request
Nor was I to be punished for not doing so.
The quieter she was, the more infuriated I became.
Like trying to scream when your voice gives out,
I could do nothing.

Okay that's enough. I am back in the present, looking at how much tinier that person inside me is, and how he needs protection, and how his pain is still mine for minutes after I climb back out of the chilled water. Sabrina never forgave me for being too sick to help her prepare for her final gathering before moving to China. I began to doubt my mum's defence of Sabrina's character. I now had no idea who to trust.

A break is in order.

Powers to be controlled

I wasn't aware that I was both impolite to—and detached from—Sabrina's friends and family; remembering being only indifferent to their uninteresting conversations. Unless the rare question of interest presented itself, reading a book in the presence of my fiancée and chatting friends was boundlessly satisfying, having the benefit of people nearby without having to deal with their exchanges. Being at the edge of a social circle whilst reading an interesting document proved to be addictive, and it kept my mind as calm as gentle waves against the shore of a bay on a mild sunny afternoon. This gave Sabrina the idea that I could perhaps keep my mind's volcanic spewing of thoughts at bay, without needing to be at the edge of a gathering with a book.

The idea that I could control the mind that controlled me was as unbelievable to me as believable by my love.

My past now seeming a collision between dreams and reality, I trusted Sabrina and closed my eyes.

'Jamie, Jamie, can you hear me.'
Sabrina's voice got louder.
'Yes.'
'How many blinds are hanging from the window?'
I delved into my mind, searching through countless images of that room during days past with my girl. They were blurry, but I counted them, one by one.
'Fourteen,' I heard myself say.
She went quiet.
'Did you open your eyes?'

'No. Was I right?'
She begged me to believe that it was hard for most people to divide a long string of digits in their head, and that the way I broke them down to single digits as though they were on a projector no one else could see was something that even she had not seen.

I was still sure she was wrong. She had to be.

Saby's first successful breakthrough came on quite an ordinary day, when her stubborn fiancé reported losing a piece of paper along with the number of a new client written on it. Jamiel was horrified. The calm, tiny woman ordered her child-like partner to sit on the carpeted floor with his eyes closed and legs crossed. I allowed myself to see the blackness before a hailing of memories began pummelling me out of reality and deeper into the dark, blue sea of my subconscious mind. Sabrina's calm voice shot its hand through, asking me to rewind my memory to the time of the initial phone call—it was like trying to get out of bed on a Monday morning, but I was there. Her voice guiding me in tracing the past actions of a ghost, writing what he did when a younger self was writing the details two days earlier.

Upon opening my eyes, I had before me a sheet of paper with a name, address, and phone number. My hand had re-written the message lost only days before. The room was tense when I dialled the number before the look on Sabrina's face was unreadable but for her glistening eyes struck by the light streaming through her living room window whilst I spoke to my new client. She was harnessing the energy wildly radiating from my head, then would be handing it over to me.

Learning from Sabrina increased rapidly from then on as she began introducing me to timing of speech, words used, dual meanings, and unexpected humour. With the latest phenomena "you tube" as her guide, she explained the puzzling concept of 'likability' trumping honesty, moral purity, direct speech, and altruism in the eyes of many the average person. With each new client combined with Sabrina's feedback, I memorised new understandings of the way people sat, the rate of change of eye blinking, tone of voice, speed of words, slight accent variances, signs around their homes of what motivated them, and charisma. The man within her boy was still in its infancy, but Sabrina was proud.

Mountains overlooking Dad's first home, 2500m above sea level.

Ancient Semitic Town of Mum's Birth 2016

Sabrina had spent months researching her own first property and when using what she had taught me to outperform her results with my first property in a fraction of the time, she saw herself as inferior. It angered me that the mind she discovered within me had now begun to upset her, and my logical responses to emotional comments were only doing more damage. Sabrina had found herself many years before, and she rightly felt she was losing her partner within the man she had helped create. Taking grip of the real world with ever stronger hands, her need to protect her partner was decreasingly required, allowing her to be absorbed into the illusion that she was no longer good enough.

'You are a shooting star, Jamiel, and I'm an old soul.'

I thought she was simply suffering from an analogy dysfunction, but she could no longer identify with the man who played a piano piece after hearing her play it once; a piece that she had spent eight years attempting to master.

The relationship descended into darkness as Sabrina was somehow being pushed further and further away. I, in turn, destructively pushed back. The marriage never took place, but I continued to wish it for the next four years.

The Second Coming

Knowing Sabrina was how my first apartment was bought, and knowing that apartment was how I met Simon the second.

A not quite middle-aged, handsome, blonde, blue-eyed third-generation Australian; it seemed the Australians I had loved and lost as a child had managed to escape to Sydney's new western edge: Camden.

I proposed that I would work for Simon, not charge the clients a cent and be paid by him. No longer in need of the corrupt Mr Chowdry and his Branson-like boss, benefitting new friends was a high like none before; there was no crash afterwards. Investing all payments received into searching for more friends, Father Simon's prophecy may now be fulfilled.

Coincidence or not, Simon saw what others didn't and in the Aussie Accent I had missed for so long, he would advise me in a way that would ultimately help him lose his star assistant:

Mate, you are bigger than this. You need to finish your study and get out on your own.' Never forgetting what he did that day, I sat through the classes filled with crap-talking future salesmen until I was asked to complete the courses remotely. Once again, I was kicked out of class. It seemed that all these years of self-improvement had done nothing to prove school would have been any different.

Nevertheless, the benefit of completing the course away from those unbelievably slow, social butterflies was completing them at a pace that was unable to wait for the rest—and not long afterwards, I would be helping people without a boss.

It was time to look for a practice to buy, and it wasn't long before I met Clive Sturt. Without the looks or youth of James Bond, he had both the accent and a worse attitude to women—welcoming me with 'Chum' and 'Lad' into his wine- and cigar-smelling office. Ignoring the mould, papers, and pink- and green-coloured rooms as I entered his boardroom on Fridays for a chat; maintaining neurotypical behaviour for as long as possible whilst getting to know a life almost past.

Another memorised phrase was needed:

'Please, don't hit on my mum,' I asked him before he met her.

'Whatever makes you think I would do such a thing,' he laughed. Would you call it a lie when within a few minutes he was flirting with my mother, or perhaps a subconscious reaction?

Me: "It's not a lie, Jamie, but one of those things people say that they don't really mean".

Jamiel: "What are these 'things' of which you speak, Adrienne, and where can I get a list of these 'things'?"

Me: "Just continue with the story, Jamie. I need to know what happens next!"

Either way, after meeting Clive, it was Mum who directed me to never to talk to him again. Far be it from me to listen to Mum.

Months of negotiation with my new source of human behaviour, I was to walk through Clive Sturt's life: how this old Englishman perceived the world, how the world had changed, how people change and had changed, his estranged daughter created during his service abroad, as well as all about his business.

He was dying but no one knew and his business—along with photos of his daughter—were all he had left. He didn't mind throwing up from the chemotherapy as much as he enjoyed the company of the nurses, having me shot forth from his office on wild goose chases along with the promise of a business takeover attached. The tiny, glistening white-haired, ex-rugby-playing war veteran who, in hindsight, could have been almost mistaken for a fictitious character that would be entertaining if you could avoid taking his insults personally, had a business that was supposedly for sale; a house of cards, gently rocking back and forth. An ex-insurance-broker, he would sign anyone and everyone, eventually building up a passive income of over six times the average full-time salary. My broker, who one day would understand his client, Jamiel, to be a 'nice, young man but slightly eccentric', had been trying to sell the 'crazy old man's' business for over three years, keeping it secret for as long as he could that I was the only person who had put up with Mr Sturt for more than a few days, let alone seven months.' My broker had exclaimed to Clive that he was going to die and leave his business to become worthless.

This infuriated the cigar-smoking, fast-walking, upright and strong white-haired man to leave him dealing with only the naïve Jamiel. I liked my broker for chastising my more innocent self for contacting businesses for sale whilst unaware that this behaviour would be deemed inappropriate and I respected him for allowing me to never repeat this error. I would stay friends with this broker as the financial advisor in the making purchased and sold more businesses through his services in the years to come.

With the disappearance of the kind broker, I innocently tolerated the dangling carrot strung by the charming Mr Sturt through meetings arranged and cancelled, offers accepted and then rejected days later. He was driving me crazy, whilst never forgetting Sabrina having taught me that this was 'the world'.

I needed my now ex-fiancée, Sabrina, with me during the last negotiation before the signing that would get me my first book of clients, and while the woman I still adored waited for me in the foyer, I boarded the boardroom with the crazy Mr Sturt and our new mediator: a mediator that stood to benefit heavily from recruiting both the business and a young (potential) entrepreneur under his wing as a paid life coach. It was time for the new mediator to witness Clive changing the terms of sale yet again, and finally to feel the hot liquid seeping through my veins after years of remaining dormant, I was consumed with rage. I started off with apparent serenity which quickly crescendoed: 'I don't know why you keep. . .' Jumping up from the boardroom table as my right fist slammed onto it, '. . .f****** *me around!*'

Clive recoiled.

I apologised and requested a minute to calm down. With my unusual gait, I walked out of the boardroom.

At the foyer, Sabrina whispered to me to simply leave. I went back in and gave Clive a kiss on the cheek.

'Mate, you're like my grandfather.' I told him. 'Forgive my Semitic blood.'

He was, as always, charming in his reply.

'If I was any younger, I'd beat you young lad!' I hated that feeling of guilt I had almost forgotten about since the past had been fading away with the help of the ongoing medications.

It was time for both Sabrina in person and Mum over the phone to advise me to let it go; destiny would provide the right opportunity outside of anyone's control. As someone supposedly so special, I was being guided on a path of world change—as opposed to the millions of people about which destiny couldn't care less.

The mediator called me as I was walking down the street, me now enjoying life without the burden of my seven-month friendship with the volatile and dying Mr Sturt; calmly mentioning that Clive had agreed to reverse his changes brought up in the boardroom. I looked at Sabrina, who slowly nodded at me. Never had I known what to do in my life with such clarity: 'I truly respect your patience throughout all this,' I said with the hope that I was impressing Sabrina, 'but you can tell Clive to go f*** himself.'

It was now time for Jamiel to become aware that only action heroes could get away with such phrases, and to remove them from his daily vernacular; phrases ever used by me both then and now were—and are—a continued attempt to fit what I thought the neurotypical would have accepted as an appropriate phase in the same situation; never actually, and to this day not knowing what connotations are attached to the message intended to be delivered.

If anyone ever had an opposite, I met Clive's the following week. Both the father of a famous Australian comedian and one of the nicest people I had ever met, he had a small book of loyal clients, a down-to-earth Australian accent, and had only just walked away from a potential buyer who sounded almost like Clive. Buying this book was a breeze.

Each day was spent in the sun after that seven-month storm with dying Clive: contacting the clients, making videos for them, and sending them financial news. Working no more than three hours per day from a tiny office overlooking Sydney with a view to the land of Simon the second, over thirty kilometres away, the rest of the day was spent talking to the beautiful personal assistant I would date and be dumped by, going to the gym, and driving my second-hand sports car. It was time to now make up for lost life by living out this new one in peace.

A few months later was when the new mediator again called me.

Clive was dead.

Clive was dead and wild animals would already be hunting the scent; wild animals like the bullies of old from which I had to keep his daughter I had never met safe. I knew what I had to do and I knew that I didn't want to. It was only then that I had realised that the mediator was still on the phone.

'When is the funeral?' I asked.

The serenity of the crematorium filled my senses with the last days of school, the days being kept company by only the warm glow of joy. With the warm glow being increasingly interrupted as people arrived, I started the unconscious habit of counting the amount of people arriving, who stood where and who spoke to whom. My intimate knowledge of his business challenged me to guess which client I was looking at, until I saw Clive's daughter. Thinking almost immediately of Sabrina, I was drawn to her.

Talking to her proved another rare opportunity to meet people my age to whom I could pass by undetected as the foreign life form I was sure I was. Drawing out the illusion much longer than ever before possible, her boyfriend was a gentleman and either mentally challenged in a way similar to my mother's youngest sister or a drug user. Either way, I liked him and was glad that Sabrina's look-alike had someone who cared that much for her.

It was one of Clive's favourite clients who asked me if I would be interested to 'bear Paul'. Not knowing who Paul was, I was more than happy to assist in any way I could. She introduced me to the other five men who would also be 'Paul Bearing', as we stood in formation, as though waiting to carry something heavy. It was 'Pall Bearing' that was needed, and so I found myself carrying Clive's dead body inside wood that felt like the wood of my piano before the whole congregation that I had no idea how to hide from.

Once again, life proved to be the test before the lesson, not knowing the politics of an estate's lawyers and its beneficiaries. I offered to work from the office until they could find a buyer and was utterly relieved that I had successfully stayed away from the dogs for now. Over the following month I would begin to witness the amazing and dishonest lengths to which people would go to get what they wanted. It was truly the first time that I had ever come to learn that many people could truly live with themselves without issue after consciously obscuring facts or creating facts if it could result in the realising of whatever their agenda may have been. It was the first time I felt sorry for the petty criminals we were forced to grow up along-side as Greenacre descended into anarchy all those years ago; who simply didn't have the opportunity that these white-collared wolves were born into. Deliberately undermining the good will of the business until they could clutch what was left with their greedy hands, my rage fuelled my desire was to let them thirst. It was time to make the fatal mistake of inheriting Clive's business that had now fallen in value three times, turning my car into the deposit lubricating the estate lawyers' trust account. Visiting people's homes for so many years had shown me the attachment they would form to material things, and the attachment that I did not—and so losing money on the car sale was a great feeling, knowing of the starving and greedy corporations that would suffer with my now new clients that would not.

Eighteen months of visiting clients every day, more homes than ever before, more friends, more lives to change. My lack of sleep and not a single day off was bringing Father Simon's prediction to its impending outcome, with the business more than doubling its value within eighteen months.

EDITH

The suicide was perhaps a precursor to Mum's two-year course in counselling, which was now almost at an end. Struggling for many years to find a counsellor that would have her eldest son's respect, Edith was approached by her student after the evening's lecture where it was explained that this student's son was extremely gifted but difficult, not standing 's***-talkers' as he said it. Edith told her not to worry, while I was expecting not to be impressed.

A polite woman whose body language was consistent with her words, she possessed a strong character that appeared forgiving while expecting much of you. Edith knew I was different from even most of those who are, and as of yet unaware how to understand and contain my emotions that I apparently did know I possessed, Edith played detective with my memory until she could find what would spark each spiral into depression.

Her first breakthrough was a patch of dirt on my pants—which would then lead to

- the tiles on the floor of a client's place,
- leading to the list of people I would have to visit in the next week. . .

  o   the next month,
  o   the lies that I would hear from them,
  o   the lack of sleep from thinking about how much I needed sleep,
  o   how I could not possibly change the world at this rate. . .
  o   before image upon image upon video would be like trying to flood water down a funnel as it simply overflowed all over the floor.

The thought of dirt on my pants had long gone by this stage.

Hours upon hours of explaining to me how each memory of mine had to be adjusted by reconstructing the English language in a way that was closer to the emotional content others understood from phrases, as opposed to the literal understanding of words I had naturally been working with my entire existence.

She explained the concept of sarcasm, of how to understand sadness in others, of happiness, of anger, of appreciation, and why the above was so important in navigating the world I had been thrown into. Edith stressed that people didn't see it as a lie when uttering words that contradicted the data I could see before me, but rather as a vehicle to convey emotion.

This could only make sense by learning to identify which words were intended to deliver meaning vs which were to be used to construct the path via words of meaning could be sent.

The above is an almost impossible task, where we as autistics must accept that the next conversation may be the one in which we unintentionally offend another.

You may remember the 5-year-old from pages past, not understanding how to look at a memory from a different angle. Edith helped me see these perspectives which I can only describe as 'changing the colour of the memory' to have its hue become a blue or green. Had I known all this as a kid, I may not have ever told you this story, Adrienne, which I can only hope, with your help, will be the torch for my people through the dark caves of the Neurotypical world. There were now millions of memories to repair, to rebuild.

Taking advantage of the supposedly unusual memory I was cursed with, Edith enabled the building of a database of rules to interpret what actually may be what was being 'meant' by the neurotypical being, and with the curse that would hopefully become a gift, my mind had become weaponised against bad memories that would always wait for the opportunity to curse the very mind they dwell within. Edith's genius created for me the 'cloak of illusion'—the power to blend in as a neurotypical, just enough to get through most situations. This, in hindsight, would prove to be disastrous as it would lead to me being incorrectly judged as a neurotypical of bad character when the truth could not have been more exactly the polar-opposite.

It would prove to be the ultimate backfire of a force that would bring the house of cards down into one, final tragedy— a tragedy from which I would perhaps emerge from, but never as the same person again.

EDITH: 'You don't need to say anything; people will just tell you everything about themselves without you needing to utter a word.' Through this technique, I discovered how to read a person enough to socially function—what they wore, the way they sat, the way they spoke, what they said, the timing of their words, how they reacted to things, the rate of their eye blinking, the level of their voice, and so on.

Using my supposedly 'Savant' grade memory, Edith dragged me through years of growth in less than thirty-six months; giving me the strength not only to save the life of the strong housewife from years before but also to build an unstable empire founded upon helping others when no one else would or could.

Again, I would love to say that the story ends here, but Hollywood is quite far away from Sydney, and the cycle of strength to tragedy would only become more volatile. Nowhere would I ever find more evil than in the corporate world, where justice is limited and the psychopath is rewarded. Learning the language of men was going to bring with it both the empowerment and the destruction of innocent people, for which I would become both blessed by and tortured with as each day passed.

Vol. 2
Prologue

Spending more time in the mountains overlooking Dad's old home was the launching pad into Syria. Being taught Arabic back in Sydney over the Net by a teacher directly in that troubled land, I had to visit her. It was time to cross The Jewel's eastern border into Syria, legally.

Driving over the great mountains only thirty kilometres from the Mediterranean, the blue and green would disappear behind me as I descended into the savannah of wines, Hezbollah Supporters, and a hardened people that were less European and more Arab; Arabic graffiti now appeared on stone walls that had surely been there longer than the religions these people held onto so dearly.

European café's had vanished along with the cheap fuel burned getting me and this rental car over the mountains that had kept descendants of Phoenicians safe from invaders from the desert for centuries. No luck for these peoples, living in a poverty I'd only ever imagined existed in folk tales of middle ages. Jamiel, the child that had been banished at 23 was back in a man's body with an income he had been saving for a cause to keep him alive. Stopping and speaking to this foreign culture forced to co-exist with its rich 'brothers' on the other side of those mountains, I knew that I would still be chained to the capitalist world back home by my need to bring these people bread. Whether she had meant it or not, Edith had affected my brain's software to come to detest its need to help others, a selfish need that I now knew would forever keep me on the other side of personal dreams with indestructible glass in-between.

Getting back into the rental before being surrounded by too many haters of the West, I continued my journey towards the anti-Lebanon mountains: the naked land mass of only dirt that rose into the uncongested sky between the savannah of the Bekka Valley and the deserts of the Syrian-Arab lands.

The border was inefficiently busy; no computers, no P.A. system, no traffic lights, and no English. It was time to switch on the newly acquired, native Arabic accent acquired with the help of the very woman I was not far from seeing. I was forced to leave my rental at the Lebanese border and hitch a ride with a new race of people that made me seem a white, awkward giant.

The sight of Damascus whilst heading down from the militarised zone was one of the most liberating feelings I can ever describe; not only was I just in a land so far away from the Nanny State of my birth, but I had just left it to travel back to AD 900.

One thing one must get used to when heading into inland Syria is the colour; a yellowish brown but for the sky filled the scenery and the 5000-year-old pavements painted with the Israeli flag upon which people walked and I would try to step around. Regular humans, so similar to my Australian brothers and sisters yet with so unintentionally horrifying behaviour. Paradoxically and yet perhaps expectedly, it was women riding scooters in the western world that the people of this ancient land would find abhorrent.

Internet café's employed lookouts for secret police after I had enjoyed a feast of a breakfast for less than the cost of a mini chocolate bar. Hugging locals after wowing them with what I explained to them was an iPhone.

I gave a dollar to a kid that seemed so malnourished I was surprised he could extend his hand for the note. Within seconds I was surrounded by children as though I had dropped a breadcrumb before a flock of pigeons. I could help twenty children before I had to escape for fear of being trampled upon.

This was wrong. So wrong that returning to Australia brought with it the pain of loving clients that had no idea how horrific it was to want a flat screen TV in the same way the Syrians were ignorant of the horrors of Israeli Flag Trampling.

Perhaps I could somehow employ more people in Lebanon apart from my Father's highly intelligent and strong-willed niece, in order to use them as a launching pad into the humble Syria. The world had to change. The world could change. Perhaps I could do it.

Straddled across two worlds and stranded in both, my mind was nowhere near the mind of Australian Customs as they held me at the airport for forty-five minutes. The rush of a past memory I didn't know I had pierced through my right ear as it burrowed towards my left:

'Geby . . . iz verry bed zat u go to zis countrry all ze time. Beeble will sink verry bed ov u.'

My dad, an almost neurotypical could see what I would not; he could see that it was only halfway there to be innocent. A human must also be *seen* to be innocent. No way could the gaping hole in my brain ever understand this until it was beyond too late, but that is a story for another time. The tragedy would take the bread from the people, the power from me, the dreams of the clients I loved and a story for you, Adrienne, once you have established yourself over the next few years.

My final trip to Syria was when the rebels had taken power. All evidence of my Australian connection was quickly hidden as we passed the checkpoint of armed, anti-soldiers and towards the news of bearded extremists slaughtering Syrian citizens far from Damascus; the very same bearded Syrians who would soon lead the rebel uprising and be depicted as the 'good guys' by the leaders of good hearted, naïve American citizens. It would be the last day I would either see or hear from my anti-theist, anti-totalitarian Arabic teacher and good friend.

The house of cards

'Jamiel!' It was one of my staff whispering to me over the phone. 'There are two men in black suits waiting for you at the foyer. They say they are government agents here to see you!'

Successful probability hypotheses of mine developed over the many flights to the northern hemisphere had brought me blackmail as well as new acquaintances. It also brought me two offices and eighteen staff. Still naïve but now half aware of it, it still would make no sense that the human's sense of probability was so counterintuitive. Nevertheless, it was my time to use this advantage to the advantage of my clients and family. Perhaps this was why the agents were at the head office doors.

'Wait,' as the suited man in way over his head scolded the child prodigy within. 'You were kicked out of the casino once they discovered that you could do that.' Now nervous when replying to my staff member eagerly awaiting an instruction: 'I am forty-five minutes away from you.'

She replied very quickly.

'They will wait for you.'

I could now see the house of cards for what it was, rocking back and forth. . .

The highest qualified professional was recruited for the job of explaining to me why I would be interrogated for nine hours in a few days. No longer believing in destiny, I remembered her as a lawyer with whom I had crossed paths many years before; a lawyer who mistook me for a rude prick of a businessman. In all fairness to her, I had only started memorising the behaviour of rich, white men at the time I had first met her; the time when my salary moved from white collar to very white collar.

She could not believe that I had no idea what concerns of the government had brought us together. Why would I. I had a compliance team for paperwork.

A pencil could drop at the other end of the office as she looked up at me and took off her glasses: 'Do you have Asperger's?'

I had found my lawyer.

SPEAKING HUMAN

The 5 Years Exile
By Jamiel Levant

Routine . . . the guaranteed path to depression.

Opening my windows to Adrienne heading to work, light pounded into the back of my skull, reminding me that the nightmare of the last four years was real.

Filling my ears with YouTube videos of human interactions was the crowd of support that got in the way of the traumatic flashes as I manoeuvred the wide-shouldered man into the bathroom to grab his two toothbrushes—one for each hand which simultaneously brushed each side of his mouth.

No planning meant no explosion of heat from beneath my skin when 'real life' interrupted. Let it always interrupt.

After learning French in fifty-two separate hours to then teach to the very same class I was just amongst, it was time to replace French with a level of English I had been desiring to grab on to for weeks.

Christopher vs Peter Hitchens was the diatomic molecule formed as only the force of independence of mind could do, and falling asleep to its vernacular for twelve months had my brain rebuilt with a language that pulled me even farther from the inner autistic whom no one could see.

It had been a long time, and memorising neurotypical behaviour was now fluid up to a point that most Autists could not access, but herein lies the reason for the nightmare: a socially blind man that can pretend to see leaves that man being judged as though he really can.

'But he can't!'

"Well...You faked it this far, you must've known what you were doing."

That nightmare remains one from which I cannot wake and brings with it the storm of a story yet to come. . .

Printed in the United States
By Bookmasters